ULTURE**SHOCK**!

A Survival Guide to Customs and Etiquette

CHILE

Susan Roraff
Laura Camacho

Marshall Cavendish
Editions

This edition published in 2007 by:
Marshall Cavendish Corporation
99 White Plains Road
Tarrytown, NY 10591-9001
www.marshallcavendish.us

Other Marshall Cavendish Offices:
Marshall Cavendish International (Asia) Private Limited. 1 New Industrial
Road, Singapore 536196 ▪ Marshall Cavendish Ltd. 119 Wardour Street, London
W1F 0UW, UK ▪ Marshall Cavendish International (Thailand) Co Ltd. 253 Asoke,
12th Flr, Sukhumvit 21 Road, Klongtoey Nua, Wattana, Bangkok 10110, Thailand
▪ Marshall Cavendish (Malaysia) Sdn Bhd, Times Subang, Lot 46, Subang Hi-Tech
Industrial Park, Batu Tiga, 40000 Shah Alam, Selangor Darul Ehsan, Malaysia

Marshall Cavendish is a trademark of Times Publishing Limited

ISBN 10: 0-7614-5401-2
ISBN 13: 978-0-7614-5401-4

Please contact the publisher for the Library of Congress catalogue number

Printed in China by Everbest Printing Co Ltd

ABOUT THE SERIES

Culture shock is a state of disorientation that can come over anyone who has been thrust into unknown surroundings, away from one's comfort zone. *CultureShock!* is a series of trusted and reputed guides which has, for decades, been helping expatriates and long-term visitors to cushion the impact of culture shock whenever they move to a new country.

Written by people who have lived in the country and experienced culture shock themselves, the authors share all the information necessary for anyone to cope with these feelings of disorientation more effectively. The guides are written in a style that is easy to read and covers a range of topics that will arm readers with enough advice, hints and tips to make their lives as normal as possible again.

Each book is structured in the same manner. It begins with the first impressions that visitors will have of that city or country. To understand a culture, one must first understand the people—where they came from, who they are, the values and traditions they live by, as well as their customs and etiquette. This is covered in the first half of the book.

Then on with the practical aspects—how to settle in with the greatest of ease. Authors walk readers through topics such as how to find accommodation, get the utilities and telecommunications up and running, enrol the children in school and keep in the pink of health. But that's not all. Once the essentials are out of the way, venture out and try the food, enjoy more of the culture and travel to other areas. Then be immersed in the language of the country before discovering more about the business side of things.

To round off, snippets of basic information are offered before readers are 'tested' on customs and etiquette of the country. Useful words and phrases, a comprehensive resource guide and list of books for further research are also included for easy reference.

CONTENTS

PREFACE

So you're a foreigner living in Chile. Congratulations on selecting (or having had the luck to be sent to) one of the preferred destinations in all of South America. While every country has its charm, the great majority of our Latin American, North American and European friends would move to Chile in a heartbeat given the opportunity.

Nevertheless, we are sure that at times living in Chile will be difficult—no one ever said expatriate life was a bed of roses. Living abroad strips away many of the things that before had helped to define ourselves—our language, family, friends and culture. We are left standing naked in a strange land and must fight to determine the boundaries of our very being. Yet there are strategies for survival. Experts say that those with an interest in the host country adjust better. So take up a hobby! Study Chilean wines, learn how to ski in the Andes, visit the volcanoes, national parks and beaches up and down the length of the country, learn Spanish well enough to read Chile's two Nobel Prize winners or volunteer to work with the needy, anything to convince yourself that Chile is the best place to be at this moment.

It is of the utmost importance that you find a social support network. Socialising with those living within your home does not count. Work or study has been found to be very comforting to those living abroad, as the rhythmic schedule and socialisation buffer cultural stress. If you do not work outside the home, making friends is a matter of life or death. You can contact your embassy to find out about clubs and associations involving expatriates from your own country, or at least your language group. Experts say it is best not to become too involved in your fellow citizen's activities, but that's easy for them to say! The circumstances are a better guide in our opinion. If you have transferred with your whole family and only plan on staying in Chile for less than a year, then the comfort of expatriate friends is more than reasonable. Fellow expatriates tend to form intense friendships very quickly, as they need the mutual social support. But if your stay will be longer, make the effort to become a part of Chilean culture. We've met people in denial. They speak only English (even after 10 years abroad) and their friends are limited to other expatriates. They dream of returning to their home country instead of enjoying where they are. This is not a healthy situation and causes them to miss out on the delights of their host country.

Spanish is an absolute must for anyone on more than a vacation. Integration into your host society may seem at first like the death of your old identity, but in the long run you can become an extraordinary person who is a full member of the society in which you live. Actually, most people we know who have lived in Chile eventually learned to speak passable Spanish, worked or studied, had many Chilean friends and generally integrated into Chilean society without too much difficulty. It is possible to go 'deep' into Chilean culture and associate primarily with Chileans.

Do not think that the person who passes through customs on his or her way 'home' someday will be the same person who arrived in Chile. People evolve, and Chile will affect you in many ways. It is typical for friends and relatives back home to see the same person that they knew before, but in reality, after a time you may start seeing even your homeland through Chilean eyes. A friend became more conscious of class structure during her stay in Chile. Upon returning home, she was distressed to realise that in the United States, "Everyone's *cuico*!" (upper class).

In this day and age, it is not uncommon to live for extended periods abroad, but that does not mean that it is uncomplicated. Most people put up a brave façade, but privately many things about their new environment are unexplainable (or so it seems), unreasonable or just plain stupid. It is easy for foreigners to commit a faux pas without knowing the reason for their blunder. It is our goal to explain how and why Chile is the way it is, with the ultimate objective of making your stay in Chile, whether long or short, as pleasant as possible. Forewarned is forearmed!

ACKNOWLEDGEMENTS

The authors recognise that this book would not have been possible without the assistance of many people. Our heartfelt thanks go to those who read and re-read the manuscript: Laura Mullahy, Peter Siavelis, Carol and Robert Roraff, Brian Roraff, Ray Harris, Barbara and James Darling and Amy Darling-True. Their comments and corrections were invaluable. We would also like to thank Sharon and Ross Gallinger, Howard and Lynnann Lovejoy, Katty Kauffman, Vanessa Chan, Gary Bland, Lynda Grahill, Reinhard and Helga Steinmeyer, Jill Kugenheim, Vanessa Friedman, Jason Kempen, Matt Meyers, Joseph Thome, Krista Schneph, Jeff Wing, Ron Leiden, and the countless other expats we met who shared with us their experiences and culture shock while living in Chile. A big thank you also to the many, many Chileans who eagerly explained Chilean society and made us feel so welcome in their country. Ultimately, however, this book reflects our own opinions, whether right or wrong. Furthermore, any errors are the sole responsibility of the authors.

MAP OF CHILE

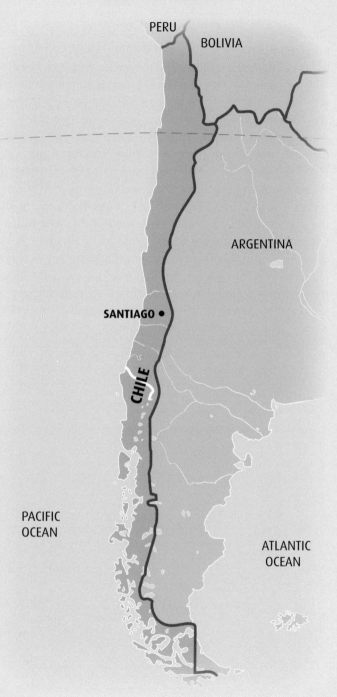

PERU

BOLIVIA

ARGENTINA

SANTIAGO ●

CHILE

PACIFIC
OCEAN

ATLANTIC
OCEAN

'Chile, fertile and remarkable province, for its Antarctic region famous, by remote nations respected because of its strength and stature. Its people (Mapuche) are so gallant, so proud, brave and belligerent that no king or foreign power has ever ruled over them.'
—Alonso de Ercilla y Zuñiga, *La Araucana*

WHAT WILL YOU FIND?

Chile is a country undergoing major changes. It is a developing country in every sense of the word. As such, it is a country that presents several different faces simultaneously. It is still a relatively poor country, with very traditional, conservative values. It is also a country enjoying its newfound wealth, eager to show off all that it has attained. It is a young country, with new and progressive ideas, pushing the nation forward. As it marches towards prosperity, Chilean society struggles with upholding its core values while at the same time striving to be modern. Therefore, the visitor's first impressions of Chile will most likely be contradictory and, at times, confusing. If you are prone to snap judgements about a country or its people, you may find yourself having to revise those opinions the longer you are here and the more Chileans you get to know.

It is also quite common to meet other foreigners who have a completely different opinion of the country from your own. We are all shaped by our previous experiences and personal values and this has an impact on how we view the rest of the world. The authors have met people who had never experienced a Third World country before. With knowledge only of wealthy countries, these people were shocked by the poverty they encountered in the *poblaciones* (poor neighbourhoods). Yet, other people we met, who had travelled to many poor countries, found

Chile to be a very sophisticated and thriving nation. Thus, your first impression of the country may fall at one end of the spectrum or the other. Only with time and the spirit of adventure will you come to really know Chile and witness all the facets of its society.

SANTIAGO

Most visitors will enter Chile by flying into the capital city of Santiago. The Arturo Merino Benítez Airport—known as Pudahuel Airport for the area where it sits—is a shiny new structure that welcomes you to the city and the country. If it is a clear day, the mountains will grab your attention first. The Andes, the second highest mountain range in the world, are an imposing and impressive sight. As you near Santiago, most pilots will point out the Aconcagua peak, the highest mountain in the Americas at 6,962 metres (22,841 feet). If you are coming from the north, it will be out the left side of the airplane. If you arrive via Argentina, the last few moments of your flight will be the most interesting, because as soon as you have crossed the Andes, the plane must make a quick descent.

The new international terminal opened in 2002, providing the country with an efficient and comfortable airport. Today, almost all travellers need to venture into Santiago at some point, even if it is to just spend the night before continuing on to a cruise, other destinations throughout Chile or even to neighbouring countries. Plans are underway to build a hotel at the airport for such travellers and it is expected to open for the country's bicentennial in 2010.

First Arrival

You will notice that the Pudahuel Airport is located in a rural area outside of Santiago. When Susan first arrived in 1993, security did not have the same priority that it does today and the fences proved to be no barrier to the many dogs who lived alongside the airport. As her plane touched down, suddenly a group of excited dogs appeared running down the runway, barking madly and desperately chasing the airplane as if it were just another car.

Santa Lucia Hill sits just east of downtown Santiago and marks the spot where *conquistador* Pedro de Valdivia built his settlement.

Just a few years ago, upon leaving the airport one had to enter Santiago from the east and drive down the *Alameda* (main thoroughfare). This afforded the passenger a candid introduction to the city. The journey began in the poorer neighbourhoods, characterised by low-income housing and dusty empty lots. The *Alameda* then passes through downtown with its focal point La Moneda, the presidential palace, closely followed by the National Library and the beautifully landscaped hill, Santa Lucia. Changing names to Avenida Providencia and then Avenida Las Condes, the street leads you into the more upscale neighbourhoods of the same names. You can still arrive this way, or circumvent the centre by taking Américo Vespucio Avenue, which rings the city. The quickest way is now a new tollroad, the Costanera Norte, which runs east to west underneath the gritty city center and alongside the Mapocho River. In a mere 15 minutes it will deliver you quite nicely at the foot of the Andes mountains and the doors of the international hotels.

The Santiago metropolitan area is home to over 5 million people and is experiencing rapid and continuous change. The true city centre is formed around La Moneda and the Plaza de la Constitución. Government offices, museums, the National Library, the Cathedral, the Plaza de Armas (main square) and the Municipal Theatre can all be found within blocks of each other. However, sparkling new skyscrapers have been built in the El Bosque area of Las Condes. Sometimes jokingly referred to as Sanhattan, this is the new business centre of Santiago. These highrises house banks and multinational corporations and the area is a flurry of activity.

Driving towards the coast from Santiago you pass through the fertile central valley and alongside vineyards and small towns. There are many little restaurants along the way to stop for lunch or tea and sweets. As you travel west, you go through two tunnels in the coastal mountain range. If you are daring and have the time, you can skip the second tunnel (Zapata Tunnel) and drive up and over the mountain on a narrow road that promises spectacular views.

The Santiago metropolitan area is made up of 32 municipalities (*comunas*), each with its own mayor and local government. Many expatriates live in the *comunas* of Vitacura, Las Condes or Lo Barnechea (which includes the popular La Dehesa neighbourhood). Other favourable neighbourhoods

This dynamic business district in El Bosque is often referred to as Sanhattan.

are Providencia, La Reina and Parque Forestal. Many *comunas* have experienced the same accelerated growth as the urban centres. You will find just about everything you need, large clean supermarkets, extensive shopping malls, mega cinemas and great restaurants.

With all of this growth, it's obvious that the transportation system needed to change in order to keep pace. Infrastructure in Chile, especially Santiago, is very good. In addition to the new and improved highways, the Metro is adding new lines and extending old lines as quickly as it can. An old and inefficient bus system gave way to a new streamlined system.

Changing with Time
Susan returns to Santiago every few years to live. Each time she goes back she is amazed at how much has changed over the course of just a couple of years and needs to reacquaint herself with the new Chile. As the number of new cars, big houses, fancy shops and exotic restaurants increases, she finds a change in attitudes as well. People seem increasingly more stressed, rushed and competitive, and at the same time, more willing to try new things and question what used to be the norm. One example is swearing and nudity on primetime network television.

VIÑA DEL MAR AND VALPARAISO
Thanks to its extremely long coastline, no trip to Chile would be complete without a detour to the magnificent Pacific coast. Many beach communities are a quick drive from Santiago. The twin cities of Viña del Mar and Valparaíso, which constitute the second largest metropolitan area after the capital, are a must see. Viña, heavily reliant on tourism, and Valparaíso, a picturesque major port, lie about 120 km (72 miles) northwest of Santiago.

Viña del Mar
Viña del Mar, once a private hacienda, began as a tourist resort for Santiaguinos and the nearby residents of Valparaíso. Viña offers beautiful beaches and ample hotels or apartments for weekend trips or longer summertime vacations. Much of the growth in the 'Garden City' is quite recent, as new high-rise apartment buildings have sprung up throughout the city

to cater to the growing number of people escaping Santiago. The infrastructure is well suited to handle tourism and there is a casino and many restaurants, shopping areas and discos. There are also theatres, art galleries, libraries and the main strip in downtown Viña comes alive at night with locals, Santiaguinos, tourists, street performers and artisans.

Valparaíso

Valparaíso, one of the country's principal ports, houses Chile's naval headquarters and the seat of Congress. In the early 19th century, with the rise of world trade, Valparaíso was a re-supply station for ships coming from Europe and the eastern United States. Goods unloaded here were reshipped to other ports in the Pacific and Oceania. During this time many British, French and Germans settled in Valparaíso. The British came not only to work in the trade industry, but also as technical advisers to the Chilean navy. A strong British influence can still be felt today.

Once the financial and commercial centre of Chile, the city later experienced a decline. In an attempt at a revival,

The city of Valparaíso, known for its hills and *ascensores*, is registered on the UNESCO World Heritage List.

the military government relocated Congress to Valparaíso in the mid-1980s, but the move did not have the desired effect. Santiaguinos have not been enticed to relocate or establish businesses here and, in fact, Congressmen maintain homes in Viña and/or return to Santiago daily.

This does not mean, however, that the city is dull. Quite the contrary, Valparaíso has a great deal of character and shows an interesting side of Chile. Although the Chilean film industry produces only a handful of movies each year, the majority are filmed here because of its beauty, mystery and charm. Funiculars, called *ascensores*, are located throughout the city, carrying people to and from their homes high on the hills. A ride up any funicular will treat you to spectacular views, both during the day and evening. Pablo Neruda had a home here, overlooking the city and the ocean. Now a museum, it is filled with fascinating artifacts. On Sundays, a huge market, selling everything from fruits and vegetables, to furniture and baby chicks, enlivens the city. The nightlife includes numerous pubs, discos and restaurants. Chile's best technical university, Santa María University, is also located here.

There is also a seedy side to the city, due in part to the fact that it is a port of call for many sailors. Prostitution is widespread and crime is a serious problem in Valparaíso. If you wander about the city be careful to stay in populated and well-lit areas and beware of pickpockets.

THE NORTH

Although most expatriates will find themselves living in Santiago, a few will wind up in other parts of the country. Many of those who work in the mining and shipping industries will undoubtedly travel north, whether it is to live or just for a business meeting. For others living in Santiago, the North is a great travel destination if you're adventurous and enjoy the desert.

Arica

Arica, known as the 'City of Eternal Spring', is an important shipping port for southern Peru and Bolivia. This city took off in the 1950s, but growth declined in the 1970s. Currently the city depends upon international trade, fishing and tourism, and is a major supplier of fishmeal, used for animal feed.

Iquique

Iquique, once the centre of the saltpeter (nitrate) industry, is now famous for its Duty Free Zone (ZOFRI), serving Chile and bordering countries. Within ZOFRI goods are exempt from import duties and value added tax (IVA) as long as purchases are clearly for personal consumption.

Iquique is Chile's main fishing port. Most of the catch is used to produce fish oil and fishmeal. Other important industries are manufacturing, agriculture and mining. Unfortunately, crime in this port city is a serious issue.

For an introduction to Chilean society, find a comfortable bench in a park and watch families interact.

Antofagasta

Antofagasta is Chile's fourth largest city and is heavily reliant upon the mining industry. In fact, mining accounts for half of the gross regional product. It is the major city of the north and one of Chile's most important shipping ports. Chuquicamata (Chile's largest copper mine), other large copper mines (such as La Escondida), and saltpeter, lithium, borax and phosphorus mines are located in the area. Although it is an industrial town, the city also draws a good number of tourists. There are some good beaches here and it is the stepping off point for forays into the Atacama Desert, the driest desert in the world, and nearby tourist sites.

La Serena

A beautiful city noted for its architecture, La Serena has been rated the number one city in Chile. The second oldest city in the country, it grew exponentially during the mining boom, fueled primarily by the silver and copper industries. More recently, however, agriculture (mainly fruit), scientific activity, mining and tourism have been responsible for the city's economic growth. It is a vibrant city with a long beautiful beach and a number of restaurants, museums, theatres, art galleries, libraries and bookstores. Every year the city celebrates the Festival de Cine Mudo (silent movies) and the Festival de La Serena (music).

Nearly one third of this region's population is involved in agriculture. Fruit, vineyards and new agro-industries dominate this region's economy. Most Chilean *pisco* (a distilled alcohol made from white grapes) comes from this area, specifically the Elqui Valley.

The skies in this part of the country are among the clearest and driest in the world. This has made this zone the main astronomical observation center in the Southern Hemisphere, internationally known for its highly sophisticated observatories. Cerro Tololo Inter-American Observatory is run by the National Optical Astronomical Observatory, an association of American universities and the Universidad de Chile. La Silla Observatory is administered by the European Southern Observatory, run by seven European

countries. Las Campanas Observatory is operated by the Carnegie Institute in Washington, DC, USA.

THE SOUTH

For travellers who immediately head south for cruises or for adventure tourism, the first impressions of Chile will be of lush forests, snow capped volcanoes, vast national parks and ancient glaciers. For those living in Santiago you cannot say you have been to Chile until you have visited the south. Those involved in the forestry or fishing industries will most likely wind up in the southern part of the country at some point.

Concepción

Founded in 1550, Concepción was destroyed by two earthquakes and tsunamis in 1730 and 1751. The city was rebuilt in 1754 at its present location. The University of Concepción is well known and highly respected throughout the country. It is the only true university campus in Chile. There are also five other universities located here.

The area surrounding Concepción is an agricultural and industrial centre. Wheat, wine and coal are produced here and the forestry industry also plays a very important role. In the late 19th century the forests in this area were clear-cut in order to grow wheat to feed workers. Unfortunately, this led to land erosion. Reforestation projects have been implemented using Radiata pine. About 65 per cent of the country's pine plantations are located in this region.

The Lota coal mine, once the largest in Chile, was located just south of Concepción. Coal mining began in 1852 and the money losing mine was finally closed down in 1997 amidst major protests. This is undoubtedly one of the poorest regions of Chile and it was hit hard when many people lost their jobs in the mine, in spite of retraining programmes.

From Concepción southwards, the temperature gradually decreases and rainfall levels increase. There is heavy rainfall during the winter months. Nearby is the Bío-Bío River famous for its grade five rapids. A series of dams was built to generate power so parts of the river are no longer accessible to white-water rafting.

Temuco

Temuco began as a fortress designed to defend early settlers from attacks by the Mapuche. Today, Temuco is the fastest growing city in Chile. The boom is centred around the agricultural and forestry industries. The area surrounding Temuco is home to many of the indigenous people of Chile. This region is referred to as La Frontera, the Frontier, because for so many years the Mapuche were able to repel numerous advances and resist domination. Even though Temuco is experiencing high levels of growth, the native people remain impoverished.

The Mapuche sell their wares at the craft and produce market in the centre of Temuco. The city's museum and university are both well respected and a drive into rural areas offers views of traditional Mapuche houses and lovely scenery. Temuco is also proud of its favourite son, Pablo Neruda, who incorporated this beautiful landscape and the perennial rainfall into many of his early poems.

Valdivia

Although the government did not offer free land to homestead in this part of Chile, many Germans still migrated to Valdivia. Using their own capital, the German population invested in industry and farming, and at the turn of the century Valdivia was Chile's leading industrial city. Today, many of the farms have become highly mechanised, producing a variety of crops. The dairy and forestry industries also play a major role in the economy. The city receives many tourists who come to explore the nearby 17th century Spanish forts. Valdivia is also home to the respected Universidad Austral. Located on it campus is a serene botanical garden and arboretum where locals go to take a relaxing stroll.

Puerto Montt and Puerto Varas

The Chilean government, frustrated in its attempts to colonise the southern part of the country and bring the Mapuche under control, initiated a programme to actively recruit German settlers. In 1852, the first 212 German settlers arrived at Puerto Montt. They initially inhabited the shores of Lake Llanquihue, transforming the area by clearing the dense temperate rainforest. Each German settler received 75 blocks of land (each slightly larger than a hectare) plus 12 blocks for each child. The families received free lodging until the land was handed over, a pair of oxen, one cow and calf, and boards and nails to build a house. They also received a monthly allowance for one year, free medical care, a certificate of ownership and Chilean citizenship, if they desired. The government ended the programme in 1880.

Today Puerto Montt and Puerto Varas, combined with the city of Osorno, constitute Chile's fourth largest industrial center, with an economy based primarily on agriculture, including livestock, grains, potatoes, a variety of berries and asparagus. Most of the milk consumed in Chile comes from here. There are more than 30 salmon farms in the area. The Lake District, as this region is known, is a major destination for national and international tourists.

The small fishing cove of Angelmó, part of the city of Puerto Montt, is famous for its seafood market. Puerto Montt is also the main port for boats travelling south. In addition to freighters transporting cargo, a number of cruises to the Laguna San Rafael and various small towns and hot springs originate here.

Chiloé

Just South of Puerto Montt lies the archipelago of Chiloé. The green rolling hills and many inlets and coves of the Isla Grande de Chiloé were the last bastion of the Spanish empire in Chile. The island has a rich mythology, which includes wizards, spirits, monsters and ghost ships. Chiloé's unique architecture boasts beautiful old wooden churches and houses built on stilts over the water.

Punta Arenas

The most important city on the southern tip of the country, Punta Arenas, lies on the Strait of Magellan. In fact, this was the first part of Chile seen by Europeans. Punta Arenas is located in Chilean Patagonia and as such has lured adventurers and mavericks. The earliest settlers of Punta Arenas were tempted by the rumours of vast gold deposits in the area. To their dismay, the rumours proved to be false. The area then turned to sheep farming and wool production. Subsequent arrivals came because of the thriving shipping industry. Before the Panama Canal was built, all ships en route from Europe and the eastern United States had to sail round the tip of South America to get to the Pacific Coast. Later migrants came to eek out a living working on the oil wells. Although people arrived from all over, a great many people in Punta Arenas are of Croatian origin. The current economy is based on cattle, mining and fishing.

Relations between southern Chile and southern Argentina are rich and diverse due to cross-border traffic of goods and people. Although the two countries have had border disputes, many Patagonians are more closely connected to each other than to their fellow citizens in Santiago or Buenos Aires.

As the 'capital' of Chilean Patagonia, many tourists pass through Punta Arenas on their way to the Torres del Paine National Park, the cave of the Milodón and the penguin colony at Otway Inslet. Punta Arenas is also the gateway to Tierra del Fuego and the Chilean Antarctic Territory.

OVERVIEW OF LAND AND HISTORY

'We will show that a nation can become prosperous without losing its soul, that it can generate wealth without contaminating the air we breathe or the water we drink, that it can foster progress and entrepreneurship while simultaneously helping those who remain behind, that we can build a country where everyone belongs, women and men, from the capital city and the regions.'
—Michelle Bachelet, President of Chile, victory speech, January 2006

THE LAND
Not the Tropics

When people think of South America, visions of white beaches, palm trees and tropical jungles with monkeys usually come to mind. Some of Latin America actually does fit that description, but not Chile. There may be palm trees, but most have been planted; there are beaches, but you can only sunbathe in season; the hot regions of Chile are far too dry to sustain a jungle and the moist regions are far too cool.

The Longest Country in the World

Chile is most likely very far away from your country of reference. Due to this distance, many people are only familiar with the country's strange shape. Known as the Spine of South America, Chile is long and thin. Superimposed on a map of the United States, Chile would stretch from northern Maine to southern California. On a map of Europe, Chile would stretch from Moscow to Lisbon. It is 4,270 km (2,647 miles) long, yet averages only 177 km (110 miles) across.

Geographical Divisions

Although there is tremendous geographical diversity (there is a saying that God had a little bit of everything left over and he put it all together to create Chile), the country can be divided conveniently into three parts. There are three distinct regions moving east to west. The major features are the Andes Mountains, the Central Valley and the smaller coastal range of the Cordillera de la Costa. These regions run almost perfectly parallel throughout the length of the country.

There is a spot near Bucalemu, south of the port of San Antonio, where you can stand atop the Coastal Range and see across the entire country. Looking to the west you see the shoreline of the Pacific Ocean and to the east you see the highest peaks of the Andes range. This gives you a good sense of Chile's unique geography.

From north to south, Chile can also be divided into three main sections plus Antarctica and the Pacific islands. Those familiar with North American geography could compare Chile with the west coast of the continent turned upside-down. Instead of forests and glaciers in the north, followed by a temperate region, and then the deserts of southern California and Mexico in the south, Chile is characterised by deserts in the north, fertile valleys in the centre and forests, glaciers and fjords in the south.

The Atacama Desert in the north is one of the driest places in the world. In certain areas rainfall has never

Chile is a long, thin country that boasts nearly 4,300 km of coastline.

been registered, although some vegetation survives on condensation from the *camanchaca* (fog) that forms over the cold ocean waters. Most of the population lives close to the ocean where humidity levels are higher.

Central Chile, where the majority of the population lives, has a Mediterranean climate with well-defined seasons. This fertile area produces the fruits, vegetables and wines that the country is famous for.

The southern landscape is more forested, due to the jump in rain levels. Southern Chile receives one of the highest amounts of precipitation in the world. South of Puerto Montt, the land begins to break apart into islands. The mainland becomes more rugged and less populated, with the exception of the southern tip.

The Chilean Antarctic Territory is roughly the same as the area also claimed by Argentina and Great Britain. While it is included on all Chilean maps, in keeping with the Antarctic Treaty, all claims have been temporarily frozen. Chile established the first of its five scientific and exploration bases there in 1947.

Easter Island (*Isla de Pascua* in Spanish or *Rapa Nui* in the local language) is the best known of Chile's Pacific islands. It lies 3,700 km (2,300 miles) off the coast of Chile and is considered the most isolated island in the world. The island was called *Te Pito O Te Henua* (Navel of the World) by the first settlers, Polynesian travellers who sailed there in bark canoes over 1,500 years ago. Admiral Roggeveen, a Dutchman, gave the island its name when he stumbled upon it on Easter Day in 1722.

Another group of islands for which Chile is famous is the Juan Fernández archipelago, located 587 km (364 miles) west of Valparaíso. You may not be familiar with the name, but the island now called Robinson Crusoe was where the real Alexander Selkirk was marooned for about four years.

Land Usage

Less than one-tenth of Chile's land is arable, almost all of it in the central region. One-sixth of the land is permanent pasture that supports substantial herds of sheep and cattle.

A little more than one-tenth is forested. Much of the rest of the country is covered by desert and highlands. Great portions of the country are not populated. National parks account for roughly 18 per cent of Chilean territory, a fairly high percentage. CONAF, the National Park Service, runs 32 national parks, 48 national reserves and 15 natural monuments.

HISTORY

The geography of this corner of South America plays an important role in the formation of Chile as a nation. Chile was founded as a Spanish colony on the western side of the formidable barrier of the Andes Mountains along the coast of the Pacific Ocean. It was easier to expand to the south (into the territories of the indigenous groups) and to the north (into the neglected parts of Peru and Bolivia) than it was to cross these mountains and venture farther inland. Although the Spanish crown originally assigned certain territories beyond the Andes to Chile (in what today is southern Argentina), the country eventually found its 'natural' niche between the mountains and the sea.

Native Peoples

When Pedro de Valdivia first arrived in what is now known as Chile, a number of native peoples inhabited this corner of the world. Sadly, the Spanish conquest, which brought war and slavery and introduced a number of fatal diseases, combined with the subsequent policies of the newly founded republic, caused many of the indigenous groups to disappear forever.

The peoples of the north, such as the Aymara, Quechua, Atacameños and Diaguitas and even those from the central area, the Picunche (men of the north), had been brought under the control of the Incan empire in the mid-15th century. Because they were organised, it was easy for the Spaniards to bring them under control.

The Mapuche (people of the land), who lived south of the Bío-Bío River, were fierce warriors. Not only were they successful in repelling the Incan warriors, but they also proved to be a formidable enemy of the Spanish. In

fact, their resistance made Chile the most difficult country in the hemisphere to conquer. The Chilean government did not actually gain control of this region until the mid 19th century.

Nomadic groups in the extreme south, who lived a simple existence under harsh conditions, were also negatively impacted by the arrival of the Europeans. While some of these groups survive in small numbers, most have sadly died out.

The Conquistadors

After an unsuccessful expedition by Diego de Almagro, Pedro de Valdivia established a settlement on the Mapocho River on 12 February 1541, in the centre of present-day Santiago. Within 20 years a number of other cities had been founded and Chile had become a General Captaincy under the Viceroyalty of Peru. However, due to the lack of valuable minerals such as silver and gold, and the country's remoteness, Chile remained a relatively unimportant part of Spain's colonial empire. Because wealth could only be earned through hard work such as farming and mining, there was no great migration to Chile. The colony's population never exceeded 500,000, the majority of whom were poor Spaniards. Chile grew into a rural economy and the upper classes were primarily landowners. However, due to climate and farming methods, slave labour was practically non-existent.

Independence

During the 18th century, a new class took form. The *criollos* were descendants of Spaniards born in Chile. They felt closer to their American land than to Europe and became the main force behind the movement that would give Chile its independence.

The struggle for autonomy began with the appointment of a *Junta de Gobierno* (Governing Council) on 18 September 1810. (Chileans celebrate this day as their National Day.) Napoleon's army had invaded Spain in 1808, deposed the king and placed Napoleon's brother on the throne. In Chile, as in other colonies, the governor called an open town meeting to elect a *Junta de Gobierno* that would govern in the name of the legitimate Spanish king. Although this junta pledged loyalty to the Spanish crown, it slowly pushed the country towards independence. Between 1811 and 1814, tension was high between royalists and separatists. Eventually, José Miguel Carrera seized power and refused to obey edicts from Spain.

In 1813 Spanish troops invaded Chile and took control of Talcahuano and Concepción before their march towards Santiago. Carrera took command of the army and worked closely with Bernardo O'Higgins to defend the capital. O'Higgins was later chosen to replace Carrera. In October 1814 the Spanish defeated the Chilean army at the Battle of Rancagua. The separatists fled to Mendoza, Argentina.

Spanish rule was harsh. Supporters of independence were punished, movement was restricted and reforms were repealed. Spain's heavy hand convinced Chileans that the country needed independence. Meanwhile, O'Higgins had joined forces with José de San Martín, an Argentinean military leader. In 1817, they crossed the Andes into Chile and on 12 February 1818 defeated the Spanish at the Battle of Chacabuco.

The New Republic

An open town meeting elected O'Higgins as supreme director and he ruled the country for five years. O'Higgins, who is today considered the liberator of Chile, was the illegitimate son of former governor Ambrosio O'Higgins, an Irishman, and a criolla woman from Chillán. He was popular with the people, but was not well-liked by the conservative aristocracy and was finally ousted in 1823.

There followed a relatively unstable period characterised by the struggle between conservatives (landowners and the church) and liberals (intellectuals who advocated the separation of church and state). In 1833, a new constitution was drafted and stood for almost 100 years. Created by the conservatives who had gained power, it established a strong central government and severely limited the powers of Congress. A strong presidency has persevered throughout Chilean history.

The War of the Pacific

The War of the Pacific was waged from 1879 until 1883 and pitted Chile against a united Peru and Bolivia for control of the Atacama Desert. All three countries claimed parts of the desert. In fact, prior to the war Bolivian territory extended all the way to the coast at Antofagasta, and the city of Arica belonged to Peru. This area contained huge mineral deposits, especially sodium nitrate. Chileans began mining in parts of Peru and Bolivia, for which they paid royalties to both governments. However, the two countries became fearful of Chilean expansion and formed a secret alliance. Between 1875 and 1878, Peru and Bolivia seized all Chilean claims,

This statue is of Arturo Prat, Chile's foremost naval hero. He is admired for his bravery and honour during the Battle of Iquique in the War of the Pacific.

a move which led to war in February 1879. Chile, home of the best navy in the Pacific, ultimately defeated Peru and Bolivia in 1883 and took possession of Arica, Tacna and Antofagasta. Tacna was returned to Peru ten years later. To this day Bolivia and Chile have a complicated relationship. Bolivia continuously calls for the return of land to provide them with access to the Pacific Ocean.

Civil War

In 1886, the liberal president José Manuel Balmaceda made attempts to increase government involvement in the economy and started a number of public works. The demand for higher taxes, however, was staunchly opposed by Congress, which represented the interests of the oligarchy. Political instability ensued. The mining region in the north became a rebel stronghold led by mine owners unwilling to pay higher nitrate taxes. Finally, with the backing of the navy, the rebels met Balmaceda's army at Concón and La Placilla in 1891 and civil war erupted. It was the bloodiest period in Chilean history, with over 10,000 victims in only eight months of fighting. Balmaceda's forces were defeated. He sought refuge in the Argentine embassy where he later committed suicide.

Populism

Despite the power of the oligarchy, workers and the newly emerging middle class were beginning to be able to wield some influence. In 1920, Chile's first populist president, Arturo Alessandri, was elected. He met with strong opposition from Congress and in 1925, when the two branches of government had reached an impasse, the military intervened and installed Carlos Ibáñez as president.

Chileans were shocked by the military intervention. Although the country's former governments had been less than fully democratic, Chile had not been subject to recurrent military coups as had other Latin American countries. When the worldwide depression hit in 1929, Chile experienced a severe economic crisis and the military president was forced to step down in disgrace.

The Socialist Republic

The year following Ibáñez's ouster was characterised by instability. During this period a Socialist Republic was installed. Although it lasted for a very short time, it is an important moment in Chile's history because it paved the way for the formation of the Socialist Party the following year.

The Popular Front

At the end of this tumultuous year, Arturo Alessandri was once again elected president. Now ruling with full authority, Alessandri focused on the country's economic recovery. However, this was accompanied by repression, particularly of workers and the left. Unified in their opposition to Alessandri, political parties of the left and the centre joined together to form the *Frente Popular* (Popular Front). Their candidate, Pedro Aguirre Cerda, narrowly defeated the right wing candidate to become president in 1938. He was forced to leave office due to poor health in 1941 and the Popular Front was soon dismantled.

A Polarised Society

With the demise of the Popular Front, the Chilean political system underwent major changes. The large number of political parties led to fierce competition and coalition-building. Alliances were fragile, and Chilean society became increasingly polarised between the right, center and left.

The 1952 presidential election was the first of a series with no majority vote. Candidates took office with less than 50 per cent of the vote. The fragmentation of the electorate continued and in 1958 Jorge Alessandri, son of Arturo Alessandri, the candidate for the right, took office with only 31.6 per cent of the vote. The second runner-up, Salvador Allende, the candidate of the Socialist-Communist Alliance (FRAP), finished only 2.5 percentage points behind Alessandri.

Christian Democrats

Jorge Alessandri was unable to resolve the severe socio-economic problems plaguing the country. This led many Chileans to the conclusion that the parties of the right did not have the answers. A new party, the Christian Democrats, emerged in the late 1950s. Its goal was to make Chile a more just and equitable society through social reform. While the right was not comfortable with these reformist ideas, it feared a possible victory by the left, and therefore pledged its support to the Christian Democrat candidate, Eduardo Frei Montalva. It is important to note that while Frei won the 1964 presidential election with 56 per cent of the vote, Allende, who had run once again, received 39 per cent.

The legislative branch, formerly housed in this building, reflected the deep divisions between Chile's main political forces.

Many Chileans speak of Frei Montalva with great respect. During his term, land reforms and the nationalisation of the copper industry were initiated. The middle and lower classes were invited to participate in government. However, Frei was prohibited by law from running for another term, and the right, which never really backed the Christian Democrats' reformist platform, withdrew their support and ran their own candidate, Jorge Alessandri, in the presidential election in 1970. The left again chose Salvador Allende, a Socialist Senator. Allende won a plurality with 36.3 per cent of the vote. Ironically, he won the presidency with fewer votes than he had garnered in the 1964 election.

Salvador Allende

Allende's victory marked the first time in history that a Marxist had been legally and democratically elected president of any country. He pledged a 'transition to socialism' within the limits of the law. Allende completed the nationalisation of the copper industry, which until then had been controlled primarily by American firms. While most Chileans supported this move, there was growing unrest as the coal, steel and banking industries were targeted for nationalisation. Private factories were taken over by workers or by state appointed 'overseers' which led to a decline in overall production. As goods disappeared from store shelves, Chileans were forced to make purchases on the black market. Anger and resentment brewed among both the upper and middle classes and the international community. The US called for an end to aid and credit. Without the support of international agencies and the lack of private foreign investment, things looked bleak.

It is important to understand the mood that existed in Chile prior to the 1973 coup. Economic and political problems affected a broad section of Chilean society. Workers benefited from some of Allende's policies—initially they were enjoying higher wages and subsidised food prices and actively participated in the community and workplace —but the other sectors of society were negatively affected. Many Chileans opposed the Socialist regime and feared the consequences of the political, social and economic disarray into which the country had fallen. Many believed Chile would become another Cuba (an idea reinforced by the many Cubans who had come to Chile as 'advisors'.) By 1972, acts of violence, protests and strikes were regular throughout Chile. Women took to the streets banging their empty soup pots, in opposition to Allende and his policies.

Escalating Violence

As 1973 progressed, confrontation increased. More and more Chileans believed there was no peaceful solution and feared that severe violence would erupt well before the next election in 1976. Rumours of a coup had been spreading for quite a while when Allende received news that the navy had stormed Valparaíso on the morning of 11 September 1973. Allende was offered safe passage and exile, but he adamantly refused. Instead he left his home and went to La Moneda, the presidential palace in the centre of Santiago. He took up arms to defend himself and his vision for Chile. Later that morning he made a moving speech, broadcast on the radio, describing his hopes and plans for the country he loved and denouncing those he considered traitors. He proclaimed that the 'free man' would ultimately prevail. The Ministry of Defense faced La Moneda from across the *Alameda* (the main thoroughfare) and throughout the morning troops exchanged fire with Allende's supporters. Bullet holes in the walls of the Ministry of Defence were a solemn reminder of this day for many years.

Close to noon, air force jets bombed La Moneda, damaging a long-standing symbol of democratic government. Allende's last moments remain unclear, but today there is a general consensus that he took his own life. What is clear is that the socialist experiment in Chile had come to a violent end.

While it is well-known that the CIA was involved in the coup, its role is sometimes overstated. It is true that the US attempted to sabotage the Allende government from the beginning and backed the coup, but the Chilean political system had disintegrated of its own accord. If you enter into a conversation with a Chilean and boldly assert that the US government was to blame, not only will you show your ignorance of the facts and lack of understanding of the situation prior to the coup, but you will also be arrogantly overstating the power and influence of the US on Chilean politics. Pinochet was in no way a puppet of the US.

Allende's memory is preserved today with great respect and admiration by his supporters on the left and by many around the world who see him as a political hero who died for his ideals. For many others, however, Allende will always be associated with chaos and disruption.

General Augusto Pinochet

Following the coup, a military junta comprised of the commanders-in-chief of the four armed forces: the army, navy, air force and *Carabineros* (uniformed national police), seized control of the government. Eventually, General Augusto Pinochet, head of the army, emerged as the leader of the junta. Many who had ties with the communist and socialist parties were rounded up and detained. Most were painfully tortured to extract information on other members or activists. Some detainees were released, some imprisoned and many forced into exile. Others were executed or simply disappeared. To the victims' family members, this is the worst of all possible situations. Figures vary depending upon the source, but estimates range from 2,000 to 6,000 people 'disappeared' during the dictatorship.

The junta dissolved Congress, suspended the constitution, declared all political parties illegal and disbanded labour unions. In order to maintain tight control, the junta restricted the media, imposed a 9:00 pm curfew and took over the universities. A secret and highly feared police force was in charge of silencing dissent.

For those suspected of having supported the Allende government life became a nightmare, but for others the coup represented a return to stability. Food and other items were once again available in stores. Many who initially supported the coup believed that power would soon be handed back to the civilian government. As time passed, however, and General Pinochet consolidated his power, it became apparent that he was there to stay. In January 1974, Pinochet announced that the military regime would remain in power for no less than five years.

The Chicago Boys

After having 'secured' the country by ridding it of the communists and socialists, the military immediately turned to the economy. A number of civilian technocrats who had been educated at the University of Chicago proposed radical adjustments in economic policy. The 'Chicago Boys', as they were known, promoted a free market economy and a drastic reduction in the role of the state. These policies were effective in reducing inflation from about 500 per cent at the time of the coup to 10 per cent in 1982. The country began to enjoy economic growth and had ended its unhealthy dependence on copper.

However, there were problems. Lower tariffs and the removal of import quotas forced inefficient Chilean industries to compete with international firms. As a result, many were forced out of business, which led to high levels of unemployment among the working class. By 1983 unemployment had reached 33 per cent and the country suffered

from the highest per capita foreign debt in the world. The populace protested and a great many demonstrations were held in Santiago and other cities, in spite of harsh government reprisals. Although political parties were illegal, de facto opposition parties still existed and were the force behind the one-day strikes. The protests, however, did not achieve the ultimate goal of ousting the government.

Politics and the Catholic Church

The Roman Catholic Church played a key role in the defense of human rights in the wake of the 1973 military coup. Although the church initially welcomed the coup and gave validity to the military junta by officiating at ceremonies, it eventually created a degree of opposition. The Vicariate of Solidarity, presided over by the Archdiocese of Santiago, provided legal defense for prisoners and offered protection for a number of non-governmental organisations. By doing so the church gained credibility as a modern social force. After the restoration of democracy, the church closed the Vicariate and, under orders from Rome, became more apolitical. But in reward for their support of democracy, church leaders made it clear that they counted upon the new government to back their conservative agenda, which included among other things opposition to divorce and abortion.

One example of the church's strong influence on government was the banning of the movie *The Last Temptation of Christ*. This decision was legally challenged, and, in a divided but final decision, the courts upheld the ban, arguing that the movie offended the Catholic Church. However, the case was later taken before the Interamerican Court of Human Rights. In 2001 the court decided against the Chilean government and the ban on the movie had to be reversed.

The 'NO' Campaign

A plebiscite held in 1980 ratified a new constitution that secured Pinochet's presidency until 1990. By the mid-1980s it became apparent that Pinochet wanted to extend his term in office within a constitutional framework. Another plebiscite was called in October 1988 that would determine whether he would continue as president of Chile until 1998. A massive 'No' campaign was undertaken that would ultimately deny Pinochet another presidential term. Although the 'No' campaign received substantial aid from international agencies in terms of both organisation and financing, it was a Chilean movement. By this time, self-exiles had begun to return in order to help precipitate Pinochet's end. Again, to say that foreign powers brought about the end of the military regime would overemphasise their role.

A Narrow Defeat

Pinochet stepped down in 1990 after negotiations with the incoming democratic government. According to some accounts, he ultimately disregarded the advice of some of his closest advisors who recommended that he keep ruling by force. It is very important to remember that although he lost, Pinochet received 40 per cent of the vote. That means that after 16 years in power, a substantial share of the population still supported his policies. We have found, in talking with people from democratic countries, that there is an overwhelming assumption that all Chileans were against Pinochet. How could anyone support a dictatorship that systematically violated human rights? Yet, if one fully understands the situation before the coup—severe economic problems and fear of communist take-over—it begins to make some sense. The Pinochet government played upon these old fears and focused on the flourishing economy during the campaign.

The Concertación

Following the victory of the 'No' campaign, a presidential election was called for December 1989 to choose a transitional government. The Christian Democrats joined with the 'democratic left'—the Socialist Party and the Party for Democracy (PPD) and a number of fringe parties—to form the Concertación. Although political parties had been outlawed during the military regime, the large parties were never fully disbanded. The Concertación chose Patricio Aylwin, a Christian Democrat, as its candidate. A lawyer and college professor, Aylwin was a former member of Congress and party leader. The right-wing candidate was Hernán

Büchi, Finance Minister during the Pinochet government. Aylwin won a clear victory and assumed the presidency for a four-year term.

Return to Democracy

A gentle man held in high esteem, Aylwin seemed to be the best choice for a transition. The president who was to lead Chile to democracy needed to be a widely respected

With the return of democracy, the presidential palace La Moneda is once again open to the public.

man with high moral standing. Aylwin successfully walked a fine line in dealing with the most important issue of his presidency—human rights—while not offending or alienating the military. His administration needed to maintain a strong economic performance while boosting social expenditures. With the return of democracy, many new voices were clamouring to be heard. Aylwin was able to find channels for these groups to express themselves without straining the fledgling system.

Pinochet continued as Commander-in-Chief of the Army until his term ended in 1998. Although he held considerable influence and was often in the news, he did not control the government. The 1980 constitution called for the inclusion of nine designated senators, who are not elected, but were named by the outgoing Pinochet government. These appointed senators prevented the Concertación from gaining a majority in the upper house. In 1998 Pinochet became an appointed senator of the same Congress he had shut down.

Human Rights

When Pinochet stepped down from the presidency, he vowed that he would not allow even one of his soldiers to be tried for human rights violations. With the exception of a few very important cases, this has been the case in Chile. Some of the most publicised and shocking human rights cases include El Caso de Los Quemados (two young demonstrators who were burned alive, one of whom— Carmen Gloria Quintana—survived), Los Degollados (four activists who were found with their throats slashed), El Caso Soria (a Spanish national who worked for the United Nations and was assassinated), the assassination of Orlando Letelier, the former Chilean Ambassador to the United States under the Allende government, and his American assistant in Washington, DC, and the assassination of former Commander-in-Chief of the Army General Carlos Prats and his wife in Buenos Aires.

Under President Aylwin a 'Truth and Reconciliation Commission' was established to investigate human rights violations and, wherever possible, bring the accused to trial. It was non-confrontational and served to defuse the issue, but many argue that it did not go far enough. A new approach was adopted by the families of human rights victims. They filed civil lawsuits, arguing that the human rights abuses were committed by agents of the state; or that the Amnesty Law passed during the Pinochet years is not applicable in the case of the *desaparecidos* because these people were 'kidnapped', so the case remains open until they are found. According to the Rettig Report (the document issued by the reconciliation commission), there are over 1,000 documented cases where violations were committed by state agents, making them eligible for this type of lawsuit.

The Concertación Years

In 1993, the Concertación candidate, Eduardo Frei Ruiz-Tagle, a Christian Democrat and the son of Eduardo Frei Montalva, was elected president by a wide margin. Towards the end of an uneventful term in office, the Frei administration had to deal with the complicated and divisive issue of the arrest in Great Britain of former General and 'Life' Senator Augusto Pinochet, at the request of a Spanish judge, for human rights abuses. After being under house arrest for 18 months in London, Pinochet was finally released by the British government on grounds of health. This case is considered a landmark for the trial of former Heads of State for the violation of human rights and other crimes. Back in Chile, he was stripped of immunity and indicted for human rights abuses, yet, due to poor health wound up never standing trial.

In 2004 it was discovered that Pinochet had secret accounts with a US bank and later investigations in Chile found that he had close to US$ 27 million hidden in various overseas accounts. This resulted in additional charges being brought against the former dictator and members of his family, mainly for tax evasion. Some of his supporters felt betrayed, even as members of his family argued that these were emergency funds in case he were to be expelled from Chile.

Ricardo Lagos

In March 2000, Ricardo Lagos took office as the first socialist president of Chile since Salvador Allende. He narrowly defeated the rising star of the Right—Joaquín Lavín. He served for six years and has been one of Chile's most popular presidents. During his term, there was an emphasis on social policy without abandoning the principle of a free market economy. Chile remained an export powerhouse in Latin America and started adopting changes necessary to become a developed country. During his administration a landmark constitutional amendment was agreed upon that, it is said, completed the transition to democracy. The reforms included the elimination of the appointed senators and greatly reduced the autonomy of the armed forces. It also shortened the presidential term to four years, without immediate re-election. President Lagos left office with an approval rating of over 70 per cent, which is no easy feat.

The Passing of Pinochet

In December 2006, at the age of 91, Augusto Pinochet died. As his body lay in state at the Military Academy, thousands of people passed by the casket to offer their last respects. This shows, that after everything, he still had many devoted supporters. Simultaneously, thousands of people protested in Santiago and other parts of the country, celebrating his passing and the end of a tumultuous era. He was given a military funeral and President Michelle Bachelet did not attend.

Michelle Bachelet

In 2006, Chile elected its first woman president, Michelle Bachelet Jeria. A pediatrician, she is a socialist and a former Minister of Health and Minister of Defense. As President, she has promised to maintain current economic policies while implementing an ambitious social reform package. She hopes to improve education, health care, infrastructure and labour policy. Her father served in the Allende government, was imprisoned and tortured and died while in prison. She and her mother were both arrested and tortured. As President she has called for the country to come together instead of pushing for more divisive policies. Not only is her election notable because she is a woman, but also because she is an agnostic and single mother in a religious and somewhat conservative country. On the day she won the presidency, Chilean women streamed out into the streets to show their pride and support.

THE CHILEAN PEOPLE

CHAPTER 3

'When the path is bursting with chatty children,
who pass by singing about the old and the new,
their faces and their voices proclaiming such delights,
I see a land whose orchards are well tended.'
—Gabriela Mistral, Las Flores

A HOMOGENEOUS SOCIETY

The first thing you may notice about Chilean society is that it is very homogeneous. Physically, Chileans resemble one another and look, for the most part, like one people. Minority groups have either immersed themselves in the dominant culture or have maintained their differences while remaining on the edge of mainstream society. Chileans generally regard themselves as one people, not a nation of diverse populations. Recent arrivals, due to their physical traits, clothing and behaviour, will have a hard time blending in. However, any attention expatriates attract will never be hostile.

ETHNICITY

Upon arriving in Chile, most people are struck by the fact that the population seems so 'European'. In contrast to their northern neighbours Peru and Bolivia, Chileans have a high percentage of European blood. Many Chileans could probably be classified as *mestizo*. Yet, although they may have some Amerindian blood, many do not consider it part of their cultural identity since they do not speak the language nor participate in the traditions. Many may not even be aware of their entire family background. Often the lack of knowledge is part of a cultural amnesia that is common in Latin America. The Spanish must accept some of the blame: there is a long tradition in Spain of 'purity of blood' that resulted in the persecution of minority groups.

This attitude travelled to the Americas even though few Spanish women were brought to the New World. Most of the early Spanish settlers kept Indian concubines. A friend once said, "If you shake the family tree, an Indian woman is likely to fall out." However, the general mindset effectively rejects this historical truth and instead identifies with a more Chilean–European self-concept. Do not presume that Chilean friends, no matter how dark their skin, consider themselves to be part Mapuche or Aymara or any other Amerindian group.

Mapuche

The Mapuche are considered a distinct group with their own set of customs and traditions. Census figures from 2002 indicate that there are around 600,000 Mapuches in Chile, or about 4 per cent of the population. In order to be counted as Mapuche, one needed to be currently practising the culture or speaking the language. However, more than a million Chileans identify themselves as at least part Mapuche, many of whom have migrated to the cities looking for work.

Although Chileans are proud of the fierce and powerful Mapuche warrior legacy, Indians, in general, tend to be looked down upon and the term *indio* possesses negative connotations (lazy, stubborn). They are at the low end of the social stratum, due in large part to high levels of poverty. Recently, there have been violent clashes between Mapuches and the police and private companies over land ownership disputes. The Pre-Columbian Museum in Santiago celebrates the culture of Chile's indigenous groups and Mapuche crafts can be found at fairs, but unless you travel to the Temuco area, there is a striking absence of Mapuche culture in everyday Chilean society.

The German Community

One large minority group that has been able to retain a certain amount of its culture is the Germans. A government programme implemented between 1852 and 1880 encouraged the mass immigration of Germans to tame the south. Most German families remain in the Lake District, especially in the cities of Puerto Montt, Puerto Varas, Osorno, Valdivia and Temuco. German is still spoken by members of the community and some speak Spanish with an accent. They tend to send their children to German speaking schools and marry amongst themselves. If you do travel to the south, you must eat in a Club Alemán (German Club). Excellent German food is served and you get a peek inside this community.

Colonia Dignidad

In the 1960s a German by the name of Paul Schaefer came to Chile to establish *Colonia Dignidad* (Dignity Colony). About 300 Germans were persuaded to move to the farm near Chillán in southern Chile. Members were isolated from the rest of the world and made to follow the teachings of Schaefer. While no one on the outside really knew what was going on inside the compound, neighbouring villagers did not oppose its presence. Many of them took advantage of its free school and clinic and asked no questions.

In 1997, amid accusations of child abuse and helping the Pinochet government detain, torture and execute dissidents, Schaefer fled the country. He was discovered in Argentina and extradited to Chile. In 2006, the 84-year old received a 20-year prison sentence for sexually abusing children. Later that same year, another seven years were added for illegal weapons possession.

The Colony no longer exists. Its members renamed the farm Villa Baviera and issued a public apology for what had occurred on the compound and have become part of normal Chilean society.

The British

A number of other ethnic groups also immigrated, integrated and subsequently contributed to Chilean culture. The British came to Chile during the late 1800s, primarily as advisors to the newly established Chilean navy and as merchants. In addition to their influence on the navy, they are credited with the introduction of afternoon tea in Chile. A number of influential families in Chile are of British descent. The Edwards family is the most prominent (they own Chile's main daily, *El Mercurio*, and founded Banco Edwards, a major bank). The Welsh travelled to Patagonia to herd sheep and have remained, for the most part, in that desolate part of the continent.

Other Ethnic Groups

Croatian immigrants went to Punta Arenas and slowly migrated north. A large group also lives in Antofagasta. You will notice that a significant number of Chileans have surnames that end with the trademark 'ic'. Other ethnic groups like the Basque, Italians, French and Palestinians (mainly Christian) came in smaller numbers. Jews also came to Chile, by way of Argentina. Even though they have been influential in business, academia, the sciences and the arts, in general, the community has remained quietly in the background. A student on a study abroad programme said that her host family was shocked when she told them halfway through the year that she was Jewish. The family didn't know any Jews and assumed they all looked and behaved like Orthodox Jews. There are a few groups of gypsies in Chile. They generally live in segregated areas and are often the subject of discrimination and contempt.

As the Chilean economy grows, Latin Americans from poorer neighbouring countries are increasingly entering the country (both legally and illegally) in search of work. Many people hire Peruvian, or sometimes Bolivian maids who work for less money than Chilean women. A significant number of Argentineans flocked to Chile following the economic woes in their country in the late 1990s/early 2000s.

Unlike other Latin American countries, Chile did not import a significant number of slaves. The Chilean economy, although basically a rural economy, did not depend upon labour-intensive crops that encouraged the practice of slavery. Therefore, there are no black communities in Chile. An African-American woman in Chile on a study abroad programme remarked that she was stared at quite a bit, but in general, treated very nicely.

Recently, Asians have begun to arrive in Chile. Indians and Pakistanis tend to settle in and around Iquique. Koreans, Taiwanese and other Asians have immigrated to Chile in more considerable numbers. Unlike other groups, due to their distinctive physical characteristics and radically different culture, Asians have not assimilated as easily. They are readily recognised as being different and have remained on the margins of mainstream society. With their arrival, Chileans have had to begin to learn how to accept those who 'do not look like them'. Chileans tend to group all Asians together, ignoring the differences between them. It is not uncommon to hear all Asians, including the large number of Korean Chileans, referred to as *chinos* (Chinese).

Discrimination

Most Chileans claim they are not racist, yet that assertion is sometimes not quite true. Among groups they have no direct contact with, Chileans seem to believe in stereotypes, most likely imported from other cultures. They also have no problem making sweeping generalisations based on one personal experience.

Exiliados and Retornados

Another sector of Chilean society worth mentioning is the *retornados*, exiles during the Pinochet regime who have since returned to Chile. This group has experienced a number of unique problems such as reintegration into a 'foreign' culture and society. Some exiles who harboured old ideas were confronted with a new and unfamiliar Chile, while others had grown accustomed to the culture of their host country. Significant numbers went to Sweden, East Germany, Austria, the United States, Australia, Argentina and other countries. The children and foreign spouses of exiles also have problems living in a country they have never known and with which they feel no close bond.

Several years ago a Korean woman was expelled from a health club because, according to the management and other members, she smelled bad, the result of her diet of Korean food. The woman sued the health club, citing discrimination, and won the case. The first racial conflict the country experienced in modern times occurred a few years ago when Korean youth gangs clashed with Chilean gangs. Authorities cracked down on the Korean gangs, threatening their whole families with expulsion if the criminal behaviour continued. The issue was eventually resolved, but not before a number of Korean families were expelled.

CLASS STRUCTURE

The sharpest distinctions between Chileans, however, are not based upon ethnicity, but rather one's position in the class system. Chilean society is stratified according to income. Notable families are firmly entrenched in the upper class.

However, recent economic growth has led to increased social mobility and some changes.

Old Money

Chile's early economy was based primarily on agriculture and mining and therefore the upper class consisted mainly of landowners. Wealth and power has remained in the hands of these same families for generations. Early on, you will notice that the same surnames keep popping up in association with business, politics, etc. Many people who share these names are close or distant relatives and these familial ties are very important. Upon meeting someone, a Chilean can form an immediate, if not always 100 per cent correct, opinion based upon the surname. Some of the most recognisable families are Edwards, Matta, Lyon, Santa María, Matte, Aguirre, Undurraga, Errázuriz and Larraín. Surnames with a double 'r', such as the final four names, are Basque names and Chileans refer to them as *apellidos vinosos* (the wine surnames) because, among other things, these families owned the vineyards.

Chileans with a name and money (or just the ability to meet well placed people) maintain their advantage through *pitutos*. *Pitutos* are family members, friends and social and political connections who are called upon for favours. Average work is quickly rewarded. Those without the benefit of a 'good' surname or the appropriate credentials must often work twice as hard to move ahead.

While middle-class and lower-class Chileans may complain about the way things work and how impossible it is to get ahead without *pitutos*, they must look to themselves as well for continuing the practice. For example, take a quick look at the names of politicians and you'll find the same names that have been in politics for generations. While family connections no doubt help a politician rise through the ranks, once his or her name is on the ballot, it is the average Chilean who votes them into office over an 'unknown'. This is not to say that these people are not capable, many serve their constituents well, but rather to point out that name recognition makes life in Chile much easier because of the widespread assumption that a member of a successful family will naturally excel.

Although some may complain about the power and wealth of the elite, the average Chilean would much rather join that sector than see it destroyed.

Surnames

In most Spanish-speaking cultures, each person has two surnames (*apellidos*), the first being that of the father and the second that of the mother (who does not change her name when she marries). This allows the public to know both families from which the person hails. For convenience, people may sometimes use only their first surname, but both are legal and are used in all formal occasions. Some Chileans that we met had trouble understanding why we only had one last name. They couldn't believe that our mother's surname could be so easily discarded.

New Money

While 'old money' maintains its status, a new group is trying to earn the same recognition and respect as it jumps into the higher income bracket. As barriers to social mobility are broken down, the children of middle-class (and sometimes even lower-class) families have moved to the top of their fields and are enjoying the accompanying wealth. This group, in general, earns their money from the 'new' professions, primarily those in the financial and service sectors, or as industrialists and business leaders.

As the percentage of people enjoying newfound wealth increases, there is a growing sense of privilege and a need to be with like-minded individuals. In the past, established families were the only ones who partook of the finer things. Now, more people have access to these enticing goods and services. In an effort to maintain a feeling of exclusivity, there has been a surge in the number of organisations that ban access by the general public, for instance, private condominiums, clubs, etc. There are a few restaurants and bars that try to restrict entrance based on money or beauty, although this policy—condemned by the public, the media and the authorities—is never stated outright.

Elegant houses located in the sprawling suburbs at the base of the mountains in Santiago reflect the country's growing wealth and sophistication.

The rich in Chile lead very comfortable lives, but Chileans in general tend not to be ostentatious. In fact, the president, once elected, continues to live in his or her home. Yet, this is slowly changing as those with newly acquired wealth feel the need to show off. Affluent Chileans, both old and new money, live in large, secure homes at the base of the cordillera in Santiago, or in other posh neighbourhoods in various cities. Those who live in Santiago almost certainly have a beach or country home where they spend weekends. They also own more than one automobile, preferring an SUV or luxury car.

Income Gap

There is a big gap between the 'haves' and the 'have nots'. While the lowest 10 per cent of the population holds only 1.2 per cent of household income, the wealthiest 10 per cent control 41.2 per cent.

The wealthy tend to travel outside of Chile, visiting the US and Europe. Another trend has been to visit the Asia-Pacific region. They also receive the best education and health care. Their children attend private schools or one of the few prestigious public schools. These same children will either go on to one of the two prominent traditional universities (Universidad de Chile or La Universidad Católica), a respected new university, or will travel to the US or Europe to attend college or pursue graduate studies. The top hospitals are located in the wealthier neighbourhoods, and if special care is required, some may travel abroad.

The Middle Class

Chile has a large and stable middle class, accounting for nearly 40 per cent of the population. Many Chileans classify themselves as middle class, even if they are in the lower income bracket. Bureaucrats, mid-level managers, professionals, office workers, teachers and nurses make up the bulk of the middle class. This group tends to be overburdened by credit as Chileans face the pressures of a consumer society. The middle class either rent or own their own home or apartment and tend to own one car. Their children attend good schools, either public or private, and they vacation within Chile.

Lower Income Groups

The harsh economic policies enforced during the military dictatorship caused a noticeable increase in the number of poor to well over 40 per cent. Subsequent democratic governments have implemented programmes and policies to reverse that trend with encouraging results. The number of those living below the poverty line is now slightly less than 19 per cent. The percentage of indigent poor has dropped from almost 17 per cent to less than 5 per cent. However, the gap between the 'haves' and the 'have nots' is large and growing.

Social Values

Overall, the Chilean people are united in their concern for the poor. Since the return of democracy, they have consistently voted into office candidates who promised social reforms in conjunction with liberal economic policies.

Housing

Chile's housing programme has been both applauded and criticised. Prior to the 1970s, low-income groups built shantytowns using cardboard and metal on illegally seized land. Pinochet initiated a housing policy that relocated these groups to state supported housing. By removing the shantytown eyesores, he hoped to change foreign perceptions and attract capital. These housing policies were expanded and reinforced by subsequent democratic governments. Residents have legal title to their property and access to electricity and running water. A very important side effect has been the sharp rise in health indexes. Infant mortality, maternal mortality and malnutrition levels are now almost on par with developed countries

There have been a number of criticisms levelled at the housing programme. First, the houses are very small which leads to overcrowding, especially when extended family members share the same roof. In Chile a relative will always be taken in until he can get back on his feet. Second, the people were relocated to cheap land on the periphery of the city. Third, the low quality of the construction materials became terribly evident following heavy rains, when many homes were damaged.

Education

Although Chile has a very high literacy rate, the quality of education provided by private schools is much higher than that offered by public schools, especially those in low-income areas. The result is a large sector of the population with few real skills who wind up either unemployed or underemployed. An educational reform was initiated in 1990. Among other changes, it guaranteed 12 years free schooling for all Chileans, moved towards a full school day for all students and aimed to improve the quality of and equality in education in Chile.

Chile is still a young country. Twenty five per cent of the population is under the age of 15, although indicators show that this trend is reversing.

In 2006, Chile witnessed mass protests the likes of which it had not seen since the political turmoil of the Allende and Pinochet years. Led by high school students, hundreds of thousands of public and private school students joined together to demand, among other things, higher quality public education and lower costs for students. The students, referred to as *pingüinos* because they looked like penguins in their school uniforms, received much support throughout Chile and garnered worldwide media attention.

Health Care

Public health facilities are also substandard, and with the introduction of private health care (ISAPRES), many people have opted to leave the public health care system altogether. One consequence is that less money is now being contributed to the public health care system (FONASA). Many doctors who work in private hospitals also devote time to working in public clinics. However, these well-trained doctors are hampered by the rundown facilities and inadequate equipment and supplies available to them in the public clinics. As a result, the level of care that the

poor receive is overwhelmingly inferior to that received by the middle and upper classes.

Public Transportation

The working poor rely heavily on public transportation, often taking long, crowded, uncomfortable bus rides to get to and from work. Since the *poblaciones* (poor neighbourhoods) are located along the edge of Santiago and other cities, many are stuck for over an hour in a bus just going one way. Hopefully, conditions will eventually improve as the mass transit system, at least in the capital, goes through a complete overhaul. When the heavy rains hit Santiago during the winter months, the *poblaciones* are subject to floods that halt transportation and damage homes. It is not uncommon for a poor family to suffer annual losses due to flooding.

Drugs and Alcohol

Drug abuse among teenagers and young adults in the *poblaciones* is a growing problem. The most common illicit drugs in Chile are marijuana and *pasta base*, a crude form of cocaine. Sniffing glue is another problem, as is alcoholism, although these difficult situations are not limited to the lower class.

VALUES

The Chilean people are often considered to be conservative, yet attitudes are changing. Issues traditionally at the forefront of debate, such as politics, economics and human rights, now compete with a wide array of topics that up until a few years ago were never discussed publicly. These include divorce, the environment, AIDS, abortion, sexuality, drugs, child abuse, etc. This radical opening comes in spite of the influence of the more conservative sectors of society, such as the Catholic Church. While discussion of these issues is becoming more prevalent, the issues themselves are not necessarily being embraced.

It is primarily the young people who are breaking with the conservative attitudes of the past. As the country becomes a more active member of the global community,

Chileans are increasingly receptive to new and different ideas. Some may be viewed as refreshing and positive, while others may have negative implications. For example, Chileans are getting married later after asserting a certain degree of independence. On the other hand, money and the conspicuous consumption that it brings have made an impact on society. People are much more competitive than in the past, always in hot pursuit of finalising the deal and making a profit. Older Chileans are amazed at the amount of wealth and the monthly salaries of the younger generation. The country seems to be functioning at a new and higher energy level. You'll see a lot of cell phones and new cars on the street and Chile now boasts the highest number of personal computers per capita in Latin America. The pressure to succeed can be seen in several spheres of life. One aspect has been a certain arrogance towards Latin American neighbours. Some firms have ordered sensitivity classes for their employees to prevent the emergence of the 'Ugly Chilean'. Yet, this has produced a backlash among some very young adults, who have a desire to return to the basics, reject materialism and promote solidarity.

Young Brides and Grooms

Chileans tend to marry within the same socio-economic class. They also marry young, usually in their 20s. Chileans used to marry in their early twenties, but now waiting until their late twenties is more common. Women used to be under a great deal of pressure to marry before their 30th birthday, when they would be labelled old maids. When Susan turned 30 in Chile, everyone's first question upon learning her age was "And you've never been married?" They found it easier to believe that she had been married and divorced than to believe she had never married. Although a small number of liberal Chileans are beginning to live together before marriage, this is still relatively uncommon. The rate of divorced and separated couples, however, is astounding. More and more, you hear significant others being introduce as my *pareja* (my mate) instead of *esposo/esposa* (spouse).

Starting a Family

Chileans tend to have children relatively soon after marriage. Since the family is the most important social unit, few couples opt not to have children. It might seem surprising then that Chile has a very low birthrate compared to other developing countries. Most middle-class families have only two or three children. Wealthier and poorer families tend to be bigger.

Abortion is illegal in Chile due to the strong influence of the Roman Catholic Church. However, Chile has one of the highest abortion rates in Latin America. In spite of the availability of contraceptives, abortion is used as a form of birth control. The birth control pill is sold over the counter at pharmacies without a prescription. While the pill is relatively inexpensive, the cost is still prohibitive for lower income sectors. Condoms are sold only in drug stores and the variety is very limited. The morning-after pill is now available in Chile, but its approval by health authorities created a huge legal and ethical debate.

Single Mothers and Illegitimacy

Given the fact that birth control is more readily and easily accessible to those with money, it is not surprising that this group experiences fewer unwanted pregnancies. Yet, teen pregnancy remains a problem in Chile, with about 15 per cent of all babies being born to teenage mothers. When the numbers are broken down according to income, 22 per cent of babies born in poor areas are born to teens and only about 1 per cent of babies in wealthy neighbourhoods are born to teenage girls.

Many pregnant, unwed women decide to keep their babies. Most continue to live at home and work, relying a great deal upon the support (emotional, financial and physical) of their families. While the social stigma associated with illegitimacy is slowly disappearing, until recently, the law still treated these children differently, especially in terms of inheritance rights. The issue was debated in Congress. Supporters and opponents of legislation to rescind the distinction raised arguments based on economic, legal, social and moral grounds, but the changes were finally introduced.

Divorce

In 2004, Chile was the last country in South America to legalise divorce. Strong opposition from the Catholic Church and conservative sectors of Chilean society managed to keep a divorce law from being passed for many years, even though most Chileans favoured it. Previously, a couple that wanted to terminate a marriage either lived separately, often forming new families, while still legally married, or filed for an annulment.

An annulment was a legal procedure that should not be confused with an annulment granted by the Catholic Church. With the aid of an attorney, one person would claim that there had been a procedural error in the civil marriage, most often, that the marriage had been performed by the Civil Registry Service of the wrong jurisdiction. Fake witnesses would swear this to be the case. Annulments were expensive and only worked if both parties agreed, which meant that many people were unable to get one.

Obtaining a divorce is more affordable and much easier, although the lines to file are long. Couples are required to undergo 60 days of counselling and can divorce after a one-year separation period if both agree or three years if one party does not agree. In special cases, such as evidence of domestic abuse, the couple is exempted from the waiting period.

RELIGIOUS BELIEFS AND VALUES

Many of Chile's conservative values are founded in the values of the church. Latin America remains one of the great strongholds of the Roman Catholic Church, and Chile continues to be a predominantly Catholic country. At one point, it was the official church of Chile, but since the late 19th century there has been official separation of church and state. Freedom of religion exists in Chile and many different religions are practiced. Yet, the Roman Catholic Church does enjoy a somewhat privileged status and holds sway on various social issues.

Today roughly 70 per cent of Chileans over the age of 14 classify themselves as Catholic. The second largest group is made up of Protestants, which accounts for

According to census
statistics, 70 per cent
of Chileans claim to be
Roman Catholic.

another 15 per cent of the population. About 90 per cent of Protestants belong to the growing Pentecostal (Evangelical) denominations. Other Christian religions with significant followings are the Mormons, Jehovah's Witnesses and other traditional Protestant churches, such as Lutherans.

Chilean Catholicism

A very important religious figure in Latin America is the Virgin Mary. She is believed to intervene in desperate cases and plead for mercy before God. Her popularity is very strong as a result and there are numerous shrines to the Virgin Mother. There is a huge statue of Mary atop the San Cristóbal Hill overlooking Santiago. It is especially beautiful at night when it is bathed in light. The Virgin Mary, widely worshiped as the Virgen del Carmen, is the patron of the Chilean armed forces. She is also worshiped as the Virgen de Andacollo, Virgen de la Tirana and the Virgen de lo Vasquez, among others.

Suffering in exchange for forgiveness is a common concept in Chilean Catholicism. Worshipers can often be seen 'walking' down the aisle of the church on their knees, begging for mercy. Catholics also try to make one of the several yearly pilgrimages or processions to Catholic churches within Chile that house special images of the Virgin or saints. These pilgrimages may require physical hardship or sacrifice.

Roadside Shrines

In the Chilean countryside and alongside most roads and highways it is common to see shrines called *animitas* marking the place of death of a loved one. Candles are lit in remembrance and flowers may be laid at the site. Deceased family members may also be called upon in prayers to intercede on a relative's behalf.

Animitas, shrines dedicated to deceased loved ones, are a common sight along the highways of Chile.

Pope John Paul II visited Chile in 1987 and Chileans flocked to see him. He visited low income areas where he stressed the teachings of Christ, the virtues of charity and the power of love. The saying, 'Love is stronger' (*el amor es más fuerte*) often heard in Chile was originally part of his sermon. The government turned to him to help resolve a serious border dispute with Argentina.

Within Catholicism there are different orders and other organised groups. Opus Dei, which has a significant following in Chile, is very conservative. The Jesuits, on the other hand, have a reputation for being more liberal in their teachings.

Santa Teresa de Los Andes

Born in 1900 in Santiago to parents of great wealth, Juanita Fernández Solar, or Santa Teresa, entered the Carmelite Convent in the city of Los Andes at the age of 18. She took the name Teresa in honour of the Spanish Saint Teresa of Jesus whom she admired. A weak girl, she became very ill and died one year later. A number of posthumous miracles have been accredited to Teresa and she was beatified in 1987 and finally canonised in 1993. Her canonisation represents the power of prayers and faith.

Padre Hurtado

Chileans are proud of Saint Alberto Hurtado, better known as Padre Hurtado. Born in 1901, he was an energetic and well educated Jesuit priest who placed great importance upon helping those in need and the social responsibilities of the Church and its members. He had an old pick-up truck and was known for driving throughout Santiago, rescuing homeless children. He took them to the home he had founded, *Hogar de Cristo* (the House of Christ). He died of cancer in 1952, but remains a very powerful figure in Chile especially among the young. He was canonised in 2005. His life's main work, Hogar de Cristo, is the most successful charitable organisation in Chile and one of the best known in South America.

Protestant Groups

Chile has a greater number of Protestants than do many other predominantly Roman Catholic countries in Latin America. Some are Anglicans and Lutherans, the descendants of British and German immigrants who came to Chile in the 19th century. Most, however, belong to 'fundamentalist' churches and come from lower socio-economic groups. For decades surveys indicated that less than 10 per cent of the working class could be considered practicing Catholics. It is among this previously unresponsive group that the Protestant movement has gained the most ground. Many of these sects uphold conservative values.

Pentecostals

In Chile the Pentecostal movements are generally called *evangélicos*, as a broad category. The name *Canutos* has also stuck, after the name of one of their early leaders. On Sunday you may see groups in the streets carrying large Bibles with guitars and accordions. Along the way they sing and recite Bible verses in unison and a leader or perhaps a recent convert may speak using a portable loudspeaker.

SUNDAY MORNING.....

Pentecostals and other Protestant groups are becoming very involved with the media to spread their message. They have been buying radio and television air-time to promote their views, gain members and raise money. This follows the American televangelist model, as many of the groups in Chile are based in the US. Along these same lines, more and more 'new' churches are springing up in Chile.

Mormons

The Church of Jesus Christ Latter Day Saints, also known as the Mormon Church, is another of the fastest growing religions in Chile. A Mormon temple now stands in practically every town throughout Chile. The church supports an aggressive outreach programme, carried out by missionaries canvassing door-to-door. The church also provides full scholarships for university study in the US.

Non-Christians

Other religious groups, such as Jews, Muslims and Greek Orthodox account for less that 1 per cent of the population. The Jewish community is strong, powerful and tightly knit, but is practically invisible in Chile. For example, most Chileans do not know that Don Francisco, Chile's most famous television host, is Jewish and would be surprised to find out. The number of Muslims is very small and they come primarily from the Palestinian or Syrian community. There is one mosque in Santiago. About eight per cent of Chileans define themselves as agnostics.

THE ROLE OF WOMEN IN CHILEAN SOCIETY

If you arrive in Chile with any preconceived ideas about women's roles and machismo in Latin America, you may be pleasantly surprised, as we were, to find that women have a great deal of influence and are very active in almost all aspects of Chilean society. The greatest example of this is the election of Michelle Bachelet as Chile's first female president in 2005. A much closer look, however, reveals that in spite of the significant advances women have made, many are content, or required to continue to play traditional roles.

Women in the Workforce

While women have about the same level of education as men, only around 36 per cent of women formally work outside the home. In this area, Chile lags behind most other Latin American countries, where close to 60 per cent of women are employed. This is not to say that 64 per cent of the women are unemployed. Many work in the informal sector as street vendors, maids, fruit-pickers, etc. A large number of these women are heads of households and must bring in an income. Many middle-class Chilenas have a little business on the side, selling purses, shoes, perfumes, you name it, to friends, family and acquaintances. Chilean women are also underrepresented in politics, in spite of the fact that a woman was elected president. President Bachelet made it a point to name women to half of the cabinet positions, but gains still need to be made in Congress and local governments.

Women tend to work in traditional fields as nurses, secretaries, teachers and domestic help. There are a large number of female lawyers, physicians and journalists; however, there are few women industry leaders. In order to ease more women into the workforce, especially women from the lower income bracket, President Bachelet has made some female-friendly changes to the labour code.

Social Services

The government and the business community provide more social services for women, especially working mothers, than in even some developed countries. The Chilean government established the Servicio Nacional de la Mujer or SERNAM (National Office for Women) in 1990. The director is a member of the Cabinet. Its goals are to promote women's involvement in society and to improve the lives of women in a wide range of areas. It addresses such issues as discrimination, job opportunities, education, family development, health, domestic violence, self-esteem building, housing and social and political participation. Currently, Chilean law states that a woman is to receive three months paid maternity leave and cannot be fired from her job due to pregnancy. Mothers (and now fathers) are eligible for unpaid leave if a child becomes seriously ill. Depending upon the size of the company and the percentage of women employed, the company must provide nursery care. The company can either set up its own nursery or hire an independent firm to provide the service.

Nanas

Working mothers in Chile are not faced with the same problems that mothers in some developed countries are. Because labour is relatively cheap, many upper, middle and even some lower-class families hire *nanas* (nannies) or *empleadas* who not only look after the children but also clean, cook and do the laundry. The *nana* is a trusted partner in raising the children and her presence is a great source of relief to working and non-working mothers alike. Many middle and upper-class families have live-in *nanas* who are available at almost any hour if need be. Most women from the lower income bracket turn to their extended family, friends, neighbours or even older children for help with young children.

Traditional Roles

Although Chilean women have made great strides and appear to be progressing, a closer look reveals that many women continue to adhere to traditional roles. We have met several young professional women who seemed to have very promising careers, yet gave it all up to get married and raise a family. There are many bright women who tell you outright that they are only studying at the university or working in order to find a good husband. Although women are gaining some level of independence, they still feel the pressure to get married and have children. Many cannot wait to be addressed as *Señora* (Mrs) instead of *Señorita* (Miss) because of the respect it commands. How can these contradictions be explained?

Certainly these attitudes cannot be blamed on machismo. For, although Chilean society can be described as conservative and traditional, there is no blatant machismo. When machismo rears its ugly head in Chile it is very subtle. While there may be exceptions, Chilean men for the most part are not opposed to having their wives work. In fact, not only does the extra income help, but many men are proud of their wives and their accomplishments. And, as some women say, let's not forget that macho men were raised by their mothers.

The best explanation is that for all the advancements in education and employment opportunities, Chilean women still regard family as the most important aspect of their lives. In the northern hemisphere, women debate the importance of work vs. family. Chilean women, in general, have never had to decide between a family or a career. There has never been any question as to whether or not to have children, even for those who need to work for financial reasons. Family is the central and most important social unit in Chile and roles within it have not changed much.

RAISING CHILDREN

Young children are raised in a very relaxed manner. You'll notice that some parents beg their children to behave rather than demand it. There appears to be a general lack of discipline in public places. On numerous occasions we have wanted to sternly tell a child to sit down and be good because the parents' half-hearted attempts had been ineffectual. Yet once they reach adolescence they are, for the most part, very well behaved and respectful of their parents.

Ties That Bind

In the past, a woman who was single and lived on her own was assumed to be loose, bringing shame upon herself and her entire family, or an old maid. While these perceptions have changed and more women are moving out of their parents' home before marriage, the total number is still relatively small. Most single women in Santiago who live alone come from other cities and therefore have no family with which to live.

Children still live at home until they get married because the concept of striking out on one's own is not as pervasive as it is in other cultures. If you are studying at any of the universities, you'll note that the majority of the students live at home. There is no dorm life. Thus, there is no defining moment for establishing one's independence before marriage. This is also due, in part, to the high level of support given by the family, both financial and otherwise. Most students or newly employed young adults cannot afford their own apartment, and there is no pressure from either family or friends to move out. In many cases, mom (or the *nana*) continues doing the laundry, cooking, cleaning, ironing, etc. Why would anyone want to leave?

The Regalón

The term *regalón/regalona* refers to someone who is spoiled by one or both parents. Each family has at least one. Don't get this confused, however, with a spoiled brat who acts snotty and is given whatever he or she wants. The term has a positive connotation and refers more to pampering. Even if the child doesn't ask to be catered to, the parents will do so out of love.

FAMILY GATHERINGS

Many Chilean families are tight-knit and spend a great deal of time together. Susan had a glimpse of family life in Chile with her host family. The family consisted of six adult children, three married and three single who still lived at home. Everyday a crowd descended upon the house for lunch. At least three of the children—sometimes accompanied by spouses—would come from school or work to eat lunch together. In the evenings, it was not uncommon for at least one of the married children to drop by to say hello on their way home from work. And, of course, weekends saw the family united for a delicious meal and amusing conversation. Unfortunately, due to the demands of a developing society, the majority of Chileans now cannot afford to spend as much time together as before, but the family remains the number one priority.

The family does not consist of only the immediate children and grandchildren, but embraces cousins, aunts and uncles (whether real or just close family friends). On

Families often gather together to celebrate special occasions.

special occasions, such as birthdays and holidays, the entire family comes together. More importantly, the extended family serves as a support network. Although there is significant poverty in Chile, there is little homelessness, the main reason being that family takes in members who have fallen on hard times. Many Chilean households, especially the poorest, take in *allegados* (from the word *allegar*, which means to put in close proximity), giving those in dire need the opportunity to get back on their feet.

MYTHS AND FACTS

Certain stereotypes and myths swirl around every group of people. If you've never visited Latin America, the thought of going to Chile must conjure up a whole range of images. A survey conducted in the United States found that the number one image people associated with Chile was the Mexican *sombrero*. This demonstrates a very important point: Latin America is not one big country or culture. Differences abound within the region and Chileans, like others from the Southern Cone region, are the polar opposite of Latinos from the 'tropical Caribbean' area. If this was your expectation you may be disappointed to find the mood in Chile somewhat somber. You will not find scantily clad women with fruit on their heads! Chileans are not flashy and to be so is a sign of bad taste. They dress conservatively, and are very reserved when conducting business. Even their fiestas are restrained. Of course, some groups, such as artists and intellectuals, are the exception to the rule. The best advice to the visitor is to keep it simple, don't dress in loud colours, get drunk or engage in rowdy behaviour at a party.

Curiously, one way in which Chileans express their pride to foreigners is to downplay their performance and insult themselves. Chileans ceaselessly complain that they are mostly a bunch of lazy, disorganised procrastinators and that things work due to last minute arrangements, improvisation and sheer luck (some say that the country survives only because God must be Chilean). Even though there may be some truth to what they say, in reality the country functions extremely well. Given that it is the best-performing economy in Latin America, how could these self-recriminations be entirely true? This, of course, is one of the myths associated with Latin America that does not apply to Chile. Do not expect to encounter the stereotypical Latin American 'fat cat', sitting behind his desk, wasting time and counting money. Chile runs well because of hard work, education and efficiency.

Corruption and Drug Trafficking

Latin America also invokes images of rampant corruption and drug trafficking. While it would be incorrect to state that corruption is nonexistent in Chile (is there any country that can make that claim?), stiff penalties have kept the number of incidents relatively low. Offering or accepting a bribe is considered a serious offence and is not tolerated. Misuse of public funds is another source of concern and political scandal.

Furthermore, Chile is not a major player in the international drug trade. It is true that drug use is a problem in certain areas, but the business of drug trafficking has mostly sidestepped Chile. Significant amounts of illegal drugs are not grown or manufactured in Chile and while some drug traffickers would like to launder drug money through Chilean organisations, the government is cognizant of such efforts and the police work vigorously to thwart such activities. The large number of trucks and containers moving through trade-dependent Chile, however, can pose a big challenge.

A Legalistic Society

The minute you arrive in Chile and begin the process of legalising your stay, you will become painfully aware that this is a very legalistic society. Chile has been built on a number of laws, each of which carries considerable weight. This is made very clear the first time you stroll through the downtown streets. What at first glance looks like a newspaper and magazine stand is actually a kiosk selling complete copies of existing legislation. When a new law is passed, these booklets are hawked like any other prized commodity. This has led to a high degree of legal formality among Chileans.

No matter what brings you to Chile, work or study, you will have to perform a series of *trámites* (legal and administrative transactions). Applications and documents must be approved by various offices. It requires time and patience. Fortunately, the government is introducing ways to make the entire process easier, particularly through the use of the Internet. Most likely any document you need to submit anywhere will first require notarisation. Take a short walk through Santiago and you can't help but notice the abundance of notaries. Notaries are kept in business by the general attitude that a document is not valid if it has not been notarised. We had photocopies of our passports notarised and carried those with us instead of the real document in case of theft or loss. To a Chilean, this notarised copy is a very real form of identification. The irony is that the more practical legislation applicable to daily life, like parking or hiring maids, is often conveniently ignored or circumscribed.

On-line Information

To help make your legal transactions run more smoothly check out the Government-run website http://www.tramitefacil.cl

Consumer Rights

As Chileans earn more money and increase consumption, they are slowly starting to demand rights as consumers. However, this is only a recent phenomenon. Most Chileans readily admit that they should demand better service and higher quality products, but then argue that they are just too lazy to follow through. The government is helping to change this attitude. A Consumer Rights Law was passed and a government agency was established to investigate complaints. Enforcement of the law is still weak and many Chileans do not fully understand their rights. Newspapers have also devoted a section to running stories of negligent businesses. However, if you are used to being on the receiving end of a 'the customer is always right' policy, you may be aggravated by the lack of anything comparable in Chile. Our advice is to be very sure of any purchase you make, because chances are you will be unable to return it. Exchanges are more common nowadays, but may require determination.

Personal Space

Every society has its own definition of personal space. Americans keep a relatively substantial distance from others. Chileans tend to have a much smaller personal space. Do not be surprised to find the person behind you in line breathing down your neck and inadvertently poking you in the back. It is aggravating, but unfortunately there is nothing you can do to widen that space. You'll also notice that while most Chileans respect lines, a number of people will try to cut. They do so mainly because they can get away with it. This behaviour is grudgingly accepted by those in line, who may grumble but would never confront the person outright.

SOCIALISING

CHAPTER 4

'Peasants and villagers will come out to greet you,
traveller, and you will see how they welcome to
Chile, the friend who is a foreigner.'
—Chito Faró, songwriter, *Si vas para Chile*

MAKING A CONNECTION

Chilean society is, for the most part, warm and welcoming. Whether you are in a social or business situation, the rules of conduct are basically the same—a connection needs to be made on a personal level. It is easy to establish a personal rapport with acquaintances or colleagues merely by being friendly and showing interest. Because of its importance in Chilean society, common courtesy dictates that a person's family be one of the first topics of discussion. Furthermore, in Chile, as in many other places, a willingness to learn about the country and its people will start you off on the right foot.

Relations with Foreigners

You will undoubtedly meet many Chileans and it will be possible for you to forge a lasting relationship with some. Establishing such friendships is a bit easier if you are in Chile by yourself. Chileans believe that if you are with your family, your central needs are being met and therefore they do not have to take you under their wing. It is precisely this emphasis on family that has prevented some foreigners from breaking into Chilean culture. Chileans show much more concern for a person who is alone, and therefore extend more invitations to those without family. This sentiment is expressed by many Chileans who describe themselves as *abandonado y triste* (abandoned and sad) when a spouse is away on business or holiday.

There is a genuine interest and an overall positive attitude towards foreigners in Chile. In certain Latin American countries, Americans in general are not well liked and may be treated with animosity. In Chile, however, this is definitely not the case. Reactions can be either positive or neutral, but will seldom be outright hostile. All North American and European foreigners are called *gringos*, but this should not be taken as an insult. Sometimes, it is used as a term of endearment, i.e., *la gringita*. The United States is often jokingly referred to as *Gringolandia*. Europeans are respected and their cultures are admired. Chileans may feel a bond with a certain country based on their ancestry. People from other parts of the world may find it a bit more difficult to establish close ties with Chileans.

VISITING A CHILEAN HOME

One of the most common ways Chileans express their hospitality is to invite you into their homes. If you are invited *a comer* or to *una comida* this should be translated as dinner. The more formal word *cena* is not regularly used, except by those who live in southern Chile. The dinner hour is very late in Chile, beginning no earlier than 9:00 pm and sometimes as late as 10:30 pm. If you have not yet adapted to the Chilean eating schedule you may want to snack beforehand, even though hors d'oeuvres most likely will be offered. The

Tips on Socialising

- Arrive about 15 minutes after the stated time
- Bring a small gift for the hostess
- Greet everyone individually with a kiss on the cheek or a handshake
- Dress nicely, no jeans
- Be prepared to eat at a late hour
- Inquire about your host's family
- Announce your intention to leave 10 to 15 minutes before you actually leave

dinner may be the focus of the evening, but it by no means suggests the end. Conversation continues long afterward, so expect a late night.

Be Polite, Arrive Late!

Latin Americans are notorious for arriving late to almost any event. In Chile this holds true for social events, but not for business meetings. Even though you may consider it awkward behaviour in your country, it would in fact be rude to show up to a party or a dinner at the time indicated. If the hosts invite you for dinner at 8:00 pm, they will not expect you before 8:15 pm. In fact, other guests may not arrive until well after 8:30 pm. If you do arrive at the time indicated, the hosts may be shocked to see you. Laura was once greeted by a hostess in her bathrobe and curlers when she arrived 'on time'.

Attire

Chileans tend to dress up for all manner of social events (with the exception of picnics). Even if you have been invited to an informal dinner, the Chilean guests will be dressed quite nicely. Younger Chileans wear fashionable casual wear, including blue jeans. Shorts are worn at the beach and may be seen on city streets, but would never be worn to someone's home.

Gifts

It is customary to bring the hostess a small gift to show your appreciation for her hospitality and for dinner (even if she has a maid). Appropriate gifts are chocolates, a bottle of wine, flowers, etc. Fruit baskets are not common in Chile, maybe because fruit is extremely cheap. If the family has small children, you could bring them toys, but this is definitely not required.

You might also be invited to an *asado* over the weekend or on a holiday. An *asado* is an outdoor barbeque either in someone's backyard or in a park. The main focus of the meal is meat, lots of meat, but side salads and bread will also be served. Only if you have been specifically asked will you be expected to bring a portion of the meal. The same small gifts mentioned earlier can be given to the hostess. If you happen to be invited to *once* (afternoon tea), it would be appropriate to bring pastries, sweets or even a cake if there are many other guests.

Greetings

When greeting or taking their leave of each other Chilean women will kiss each other once on the right cheek. Men and women do the same when arriving or leaving. Men shake hands with each other, although close friends may shake hands and embrace (*un abrazo*). These greetings are common only in social situations and may not be appropriate in business settings depending upon the relationship. Even if there are 20 people at the party, Chileans will still make the rounds greeting everyone individually. Only when attending a very large, noisy party will you be exempt from doing so.

In Chile, it is common for close friends greet each other with an *abrazo*.

When you are ready to leave mention that you must be going, but do not jump up and bolt out the door. The first time you state your intention it is merely a warning that you will be leaving soon. Conversation should continue for about 10 to 15 minutes longer. After such time, you can stand up, state that you really must be going and ask for your coat. You may, however, find it difficult to disengage yourself from the conversation. There is a running joke in Chile that friends continue to chat even after the car has pulled away and is driving down the street. If you have your own car, it would be appropriate and greatly appreciated if you offered a ride to anyone without one, regardless of whether it is on your way home or not. If you do not have a way home, don't be surprised if someone you just met offers you a ride. This is part of Chilean hospitality.

Don't Look The Other Way

On the surface, Chileans may appear to be more outgoing than perhaps your fellow countrymen. Once you have met someone, they will go out of their way to greet you if you happen upon each other on the street or at another function. We know of many Americans who have pretended not to notice someone for fear of becoming involved in a long-drawn-out conversation. Chileans, like all Latinos, do just the opposite and will track you down to say hello and ask how you are doing, even if it is just for a second. Susan once was sitting in a running car waiting to pick up her husband when a friend passed by. Instead of just waving, he walked all the way over to the car just to greet her with a kiss on the cheek and say hello. Yes, it can be time-consuming, but it is a very nice gesture that makes you feel well liked, respected and appreciated. If you run into someone you know, you'd be better off in the long run stopping and chatting than being caught trying to avoid recognition.

These gestures are really quite nice and attest to a more relaxed form of visiting that might be lost in the hectic pace of other societies. Greeting everyone individually allows you to take a moment and learn people's names and how they know the host. You then feel more comfortable and can enjoy everyone's company. Mentioning that you need to leave before you actually do, lets the host know that you are having a great time and need to leave but find it hard to be pulled away. Susan returned to the United States and felt slightly insulted when in the middle of a seemingly good time her guests said they had to leave, jumped up and were out the door in three minutes.

Conversation

In general, conversations at dinners and parties in Chile are not that different from those in many other countries. Conversation will usually begin with your family, i.e., children, siblings, parents, etc. and their occupations. You should show similar interest in the families of the hosts and other guests. People will also be curious as to why you are in Chile, your profession and where and what you studied. Naturally they will be interested in your impressions of their country and whether you've had a chance to travel. Chileans are very proud and will wholeheartedly agree with compliments you make regarding the economic progress and physical beauty of the country. You may find Chileans more critical of other aspects of life in Chile, however, and they will be interested to know how life in Chile compares to life in your home country. Chileans tend to be self-deprecating, often making jokes about what a backward country Chile is or how dishonest their fellow Chileans are. You are not expected to agree with these claims wholeheartedly.

Chileans are not generally concerned with keeping the conversation 'politically correct'. When speaking about other groups of people, whether from different cultures or of a different sexual orientation, some comments may appear harsh, insensitive and derogatory. Most Chileans firmly believe that they are not racists, but then make conflicting, sometimes shocking, statements without realising the obvious contradictions. You'll often hear, "I'm not racist, but..."

There is also a tendency for some Chileans to look down on indigenous groups within the country. This attitude lingers in spite of the higher standing these groups have achieved as part of an overall growing interest in environmental and indigenous issues. The terms *indio* and *cholo* in reference to the native population carry negative connotations, and although they are commonly used, we would suggest that you refrain from including them in your vocabulary.

Another topic often introduced is body weight. It is not considered rude to remark on someone's weight gain or loss. It is not meant as an insult, merely an observation. In fact, this is true with many other physical attributes, for example, hairstyles. If you are unfortunate enough to get a really bad haircut, no one will lie to make you feel better. A friend was once asked if someone had cut his hair with an axe. Although he understood Chilean culture quite well and knew it was not meant as an insult, he was nevertheless hurt by her candid remarks. The same Chilean also told him that a friend of his was quite ugly. The best advice is to just ignore the comment because there is no malice intended.

On the other hand, you'll know that a compliment is heartfelt and not meant to make you feel better. Chileans can also be equally blunt about your Spanish-speaking capabilities, although they will continuously encourage you to practice and are more than willing to help. Chileans are flattered when a foreigner attempts to learn Spanish and they often excitedly explain the intricacies of Chilean slang.

It is not acceptable to discuss salaries unless you are among very close friends. It is fine to ask how much an impersonal item cost, such as a major appliance, but you should refrain from asking about the cost of more personal items such as jewellery. Chileans are more relaxed when discussing rent.

Rude Behaviour

Always cover your mouth while yawning. Holding your hand palm up, fingers curled as if you're holding an apple is an extremely insulting and obscene gesture. Chewing gum is not appropriate in a formal situation. Hats should never be worn indoors and it is rude to walk around barefoot inside someone's home. According to superstition, a woman should never set her purse on the floor as this will cause her to lose money.

Do not expect to watch television when visiting Chileans in their home. Upon entering the living room you may be struck by the feeling that something is missing. In most Chilean homes, televisions are in the bedrooms. Living rooms are for visiting only. If you become close friends with someone, you may be invited into the bedroom to watch television. This invitation, in most instances, is perfectly innocent and should not be misconstrued. Larger new homes now include a family room, where a common TV can be found.

Hopefully you'll be invited to an *asado*, where Chileans celebrate fiestas, holidays, birthdays and sometimes just a warm summer day.

INVITING CHILEANS TO YOUR HOME

At some point in your stay you most likely will find it necessary to invite some Chileans to your home. If you remember the points above, you should do just fine. Expect them to arrive a few minutes late and do not be offended. Do not invite them over too early in the evening, because they most likely will show up later anyhow. Eight o'clock or later is a good time for an invitation. Drinks and hors d'oeuvres should be followed by dinner, either sit down or buffet style depending on the number of people invited. Coffee and tea should be served only after dessert has been finished. Offer after dinner drinks and sit back and enjoy the company because your guests most likely will stay for awhile.

Smoking

Chileans are heavy smokers, especially the women. Smoking is allowed in almost all public places. If you come from a country with stringent no-smoking policies, your lungs will have to adjust. Many people smoke in offices and restaurants (which are not divided into smoking and non-smoking sections) and do not feel uncomfortable lighting up in someone else's home. Yet, if you specifically ask them to refrain from smoking in your home they will honour your request and smoke outside or on the terrace.

Eating Out

Chileans are becoming more sophisticated and more adventurous when it comes to food. New interesting and exotic restaurants have sprung up all over the country, especially in Santiago. Areas of the city that have a good selection of restaurants are Plaza Peru in El Bosque Norte, Avenida Las Condes and Borderío in Vitacura.

INVITATIONS TO DINE OUT

It is not entirely uncommon to be invited out to dinner at a restaurant instead of someone's home. The issue of who pays the bill should be clear by the nature of the invitation. If the invitation is very casual, most likely everyone will pay for themselves. Chileans will not squabble over exact amounts, so bills are split evenly. If you order only a soup to try and save money, your plan may backfire. A foreigner being invited out for the first time will often be treated to dinner. Also, a single woman will not be expected to pay. If you invite someone out to dinner, you should pick up the check.

If you invite Chilean friends or colleagues over for dinner or out to a restaurant and they decline, you might find their excuse somewhat questionable. Do not worry that they don't like you or were trying to find a way out of spending an evening with you. They most likely have a very legitimate reason for not attending, but in their minds, it is better to tell a few half-truths than to be honest.

NIGHTLIFE

Instead of a quiet dinner, you might want to explore the nightlife scene. There are discos, bars and clubs for different ages and music tastes in every city. In Santiago there are several very good spots. A familiar neighbourhood is Bellavista, a trendy, bohemian area with restaurants, theatres, discos and bars, some with live bands. The Suecia area in Providencia offers much of the same, but is not as artsy. There are huge discos hidden on the outskirts of Santiago. The more underground, cutting edge discos are in industrial areas or warehouses and you need to know the right people to find out the locations. You have to be a night owl to put on your dancing shoes since the discos open around midnight and stay open until 5:00 am!

A Changing Scene

As recently as a few years ago, women would not venture out to the bars or discos if not in the company of a man, whether as part of a couple or group. Women did not even go out on the town alone in large numbers because this was viewed as scandalous and inappropriate behaviour. However, this has changed and you will now see groups of women out on the town. Along with this new sense of independence, there is a growing demand for respect and equality. In a well-publicised case five women successfully sued a restaurant for discrimination.

In spite of the social changes, chivalry is alive and well. When women and men go out for the evening, whether as friends or as a couple, the women are often escorted home. Santiago is no less safe than most large cities, so this is not done purely for safety reasons, it is just considered gentlemanly behaviour, like opening doors. When women and men go out together in groups as friends, the women may or may not be expected to pay for themselves. If a woman is invited out on a date with a man, she will not be expected to pay at all. Chilean women will not offer to pay, but if a foreign woman insists on paying, the man will politely but adamantly refuse her request.

POLOLOS

Dating in Chile is a very serious undertaking. Single Chileans either have a *pololo* (boyfriend) or *polola* (girlfriend) or are not seeing anyone. It is not common for Chileans to date casually or to date more than one person at a time. Although the younger generation may be more open to casual dating, many still form serious relationship rather quickly. The word *pololo* comes from the name of a bug that buzzes around people incessantly.

The majority of couples meet through friends, at school or at work. By the time they finally go out in a romantic setting, it is fairly clear that a serious relationship is being formed. Once a couple is officially a couple the relationship becomes very intense and possessive. Couples will likely spend all their free time together. If they see their friends, they do so as a couple as opposed to going out with just the girls or just the guys.

Coming from a different culture, these relationships could be described as suffocating and might offer an explanation for the relatively high number of failed marriages and adulterous affairs. The choice appears to be either to have no romantic life at all or to enter into a very serious relationship. There is no middle road.

Couples tend to be very affectionate in public. Young couples hold hands, embrace and kiss passionately whether at a restaurant, the movies or just out walking around. If you come from a more reserved country you will have to get used to this practice. Some couples can be particularly hard to ignore, but giving them dirty looks will not cause them to change their behaviour. Because most young couples live at home, they have no private areas where they can be intimate. As a result, parks, particularly Santa Lucia Hill or Parque Forestal in Santiago, have become a meeting place for countless amorous couples. In fact, in the small town of Pichidangui, there is a space among the rocks along the coastline commonly known as *la cuna* (the cradle). It is a comfortable space for two people to lie in without being seen. The name refers to the number of babies conceived here.

Hotels and Motels

The difference between a hotel and a motel in Chile is not so simple. A hotel is a hotel, but a motel—unless clearly marked *motel de turismo*—is strictly for lovers. Since many people lived with their parents until they got married, couples needed a place to go to be intimate. People having affairs also needed somewhere private to go. These needs were met by the motels. It is quite a fascinating set-up. Upon entering a motel in your car, you see no one and no one sees you. A voice tells you which room is yours and the door is opened. After parking, a huge curtain is pulled closed, hiding your car so that other patrons will not recognise it or note your license plate number. Once in the room, you order room service and pay through a revolving window in the wall. Some motels are just rooms, others have hot tubs, heart shaped beds, porn, etc.

In Santiago, the most famous and expensive motel is the Valdivia downtown. It is customary for newlyweds to go there

Make sure you know the difference between a hotel and a motel!

for their honeymoon. Motels are openly recognised for what they are and are used as landmarks. Laura once lived two houses away from a motel and everyone, from old ladies to children, knew where it was. Of course, most raised their eyebrows and joked about her being able to see whose cars went in and out.

ALTERNATIVE LIFESTYLES

Chile is still a conservative country and while homosexuality may be gaining acceptance, it is slow in coming. Many Chileans, primarily those over the age of 40, maintain attitudes that are stuck in the past. The non-judgmental term, *homosexual*, is almost never used by Chileans, who seem to prefer the derogatory *maricón* or *fleto*. The neutral English term 'gay' is being used more frequently. Among the younger generations there is less outright condemnation, but there are whispers and pointing. With the exception of artists, gays remain in the closet. It would be rare to meet an openly gay couple. However, the gay and lesbian scene is quietly active and growing. There are a number of clubs throughout Santiago where gays and lesbians can go have fun and feel comfortable and safe.

RITUALS

One of the most interesting things about living abroad is to see how others celebrate the same important moments in life. Hopefully, you'll be invited to share one of these special occasions with new friends. Many of the rituals that Chileans observe are religious in nature and are based on long-standing traditions. Even Chileans who do not attend church services on a regular basis celebrate major events in the church, such as baptisms, weddings and funerals.

Baptism

When a child is approximately six months old, he or she will be baptised. In the cities, this is a relatively quiet affair. The child is baptised by a priest in the parent's parish church and two very close family members or friends serve as the *padrinos de bautismo* (godparents). Following the church service, all guests proceed to the family's home for a long lunch or tea. Gifts are given that may be religious in nature or not. In rural areas, however, the baptism of a newborn can be a much more elaborate affair. The event can last the entire day, beginning with an *asado*. The food and drinks are abundant and the atmosphere is festive.

In the past, gifts were never given before the birth of the child. (This practice was a hold over from the days when a newborn's chance of survival was less assured.) Only recently have baby showers started to catch on in Chile. However, if a friend or close acquaintance is pregnant and you are not aware of any baby shower, you should wait until the baby is born to give your gift.

First Communion

A child receives his or her First Communion around the age of eight. The child is guided by *padrinos de comunión*, close friends or family members chosen by the parents. Boys dress up in suits and girls wear white dresses with veils. Following the church service lunch or tea is served at the family's home and gifts are given. Once again they may be religious in nature or not. Many children receive their First Communion on 8 December, the Feast of the Immaculate Conception.

Birthdays

Chileans celebrate birthdays with parties or small family gatherings. Young children normally will be given parties at home with cousins and/or friends. However, with the growing number of fast food outlets, children's parties are increasingly held at McDonald's, Chuck E. Cheese (a pizza parlour with games and shows for children) or some similar venue. Adults usually celebrate at someone's home. Gifts are opened during the party after the cake is cut. If attending a birthday party for an adult, always bring a gift, even if it is just a small token. When the host dims the lights you know it's time for the cake to be brought out. Everyone sings the Chilean version of *Happy Birthday*. So that you can sing along, the words are as follows: "*Cumpleaños Feliz; Te deseamos a ti; Cumpleaños* (insert name); *Que los cumplas feliz.*"

Saint's Day

In addition to birthdays, many Chileans celebrate their Saint's Day. Each saint is honoured on a certain day of the year according to the Catholic calendar and Chileans celebrate the day of the Saint for whom they are named. This practice is kept mainly by older Chileans. However, Chileans named after very popular saints, such as Pedro (Peter) and Pablo (Paul) celebrate their Saint's Day regardless of their age. Those who observe their Saint's Day do so in a manner similar to that of celebrating a birthday. There are cakes and presents at a small party or family gathering. Those who do not have a formal celebration, will at least receive well wishes on this day.

Although the law in Chile requires only a civil ceremony, many couples do not consider themselves truly married until after the religious ceremony.

Weddings

In Chile, the civil marriage, or legal aspect of the union, is completely separate from the religious ceremony. For those couples who wish to get married in a religious ceremony, they must also either get married in a civil ceremony or visit the Civil Registry both before and after the religious ceremony in order to have their marriage ratified. Couples who have two ceremonies celebrate the date of the religious ceremony as their wedding anniversary.

Civil Ceremony

Almost all couples are married by an official from the Civil Registry in a legal ceremony, regardless of whether or not they have a religious ceremony. This is a short ceremony…

Types of Marriages

The official will ask how the couple wishes to be married.

In Chile, there are three different legal forms of marriage:

■ *Sociedad Conyugal (this is the most common type of marriage)* According to this type of marriage all property is considered jointly owned;

■ *Separación Total de Bienes* (Divided Property) Under this type of marriage what each person owns and earns remains separate property. This is the form most often chosen;

■ Assets acquired prior to marriage remain separate, while those acquired during the marriage become common property.

After the couple gives their consent to be married, they sign the civil registry records and are given a *Libreta de Familia* (Family Book). The marriage of the couple is legally recorded in this book, which also has pages to record the birth and death of any children and the deaths of the husband and wife. This *libreta* is independent of any certificate, but summarises the history of the family. In addition to being a useful tool in completing transactions, such as school registration, it is an important symbol, because it is proof of a formal, legal relationship. In most families, it is the woman who guards the *libreta* because it is a source of pride and gives legal status to her family. A common joke says that women will only sleep with a man *con libreta* (with the book).

The civil ceremony is very simple, the men wear suits and the women wear dresses, not bridal gowns. The offices are small, so only the couple, the witnesses and maybe the parents are present. Following the ceremony, the couple, accompanied by family and intimate friends, enjoys a celebratory lunch.

Religious Ceremony

As little as a few days to as many as a few months following the civil ceremony, the couple may choose to be married in a religious service. This is the 'real' wedding, in the sense that the bride wears a white gown, the church is filled with flowers and music, and the reception comes complete with food and dancing. Most weddings are held in the evening, around 8:00 pm, on a Saturday. In the Catholic Church a full mass is not celebrated, just a short 20-minute wedding ceremony with Communion. In Chile, there are no 'wedding parties', i.e. bridesmaids or groomsmen. Instead, the bride and groom are each accompanied by *padrinos de matrimonio*—a *madrina* (a woman) and a *padrino* (a man) who stand beside them and pledge to support them in their future life together. Most often the parents are asked to be the *padrinos de matrimonio*. However, if a parent is absent, another close relative or close friend may be asked.

Following the church service, everyone is invited to a reception. This may be at a restaurant, a *casa de eventos* (rental hall) or a private home. After greeting their guests, the couple will dance their first dance together, the *Blue Danube Waltz* by Johann Strauss. After dinner, the couple will cut the cake, the bride will toss her bouquet and the groom will remove her garter and throw it to the single men. The dancing and partying will continue for a few hours.

Chileans do not give money as a wedding gift. This would imply that no thought was given to selecting a present for the newlyweds. Even gift certificates are considered inappropriate. Most couples receive traditional wedding gifts, mainly household items. Increasingly couples are registering at major department stores for specific gifts to make it easier for their guests. These stores publish *Listas de Novios* (lists of engaged couples) in the paper on a regular basis.

Funerals

Following a death, a wake and funeral will be held at the church on the same day. Because the body is not normally embalmed, the funeral is held shortly after the death. Very close friends and extended family often arrive at the church a few hours prior to the service to provide support. The immediate family will observe a certain period of external mourning, but this practice is more obvious in the countryside and among very traditional families. Today, it is a matter of personal choice whether or not to dress in black for an extended period.

Old style mausoleums like this one, are being rapidly replaced by park-like cemeteries.

One month following the death of a loved one and then every year on the anniversary of the death, a full Catholic mass may be offered in the deceased's memory. Other families may opt to offer their prayers in silence. On 1 November, All Saints' Day, family members go to the cemetery to visit the grave of a loved one.

In the past, the remains were interred in mausoleum type concrete blocks. Only the wealthy could afford graves in the ground. A common practice was to remove the remains of a spouse from the mausoleum after a period of time, place them in an urn and return them to the mausoleum. This allowed both spouses to be buried together. Newer cemeteries tend to offer graves in the ground.

Many people send flowers when a person has died to offer their condolences. A growing number of people now prefer to make a donation to charity in memory of the deceased. The charity then sends a sympathy card with the name of the donor to the family. An obituary is placed in the paper to announce a person's death. Friends may take out their own notices in the paper to remember the deceased.

In rural areas funerals can be a much more involved affair. The wake itself can last for a few days, either at the deceased's home or the local church. Many mourners bring food and the eating continues until the funeral takes place. In the event that a baby has died, the mourners sometimes hold a *Velorio del Angelito* (Little Angel's Wake). It is widely believed that the baby will go straight to heaven, so it cannot be a mournful event.

SETTLING IN

CHAPTER 5

'*Estar más perdido que el Teniente Bello.*'
(To be more lost than Lieutenant Bello.)
—Chilean saying, inspired by an army pilot who
disappeared on a mission and was never found again

WELCOME TO SANTIAGO

If you've made the decision to move to Chile, you are in for a wonderful experience. However, some adjustments will be necessary with respect to day-to-day living. Because most expatriates will be living in Santiago, this chapter will focus on the capital. However, much of the information that follows holds true for all of Chile.

Santiago is a sprawling metropolis. Roughly one-third of the country's population of 16 million lives here. The city is growing up into the foothills of the Andes Mountains to the east, as well as to the north, south and west. The more affluent Santiaguinos began moving closer and closer to the base of the *cordillera* (mountain range) in increasing numbers in the early 1980s. It was during this time that new neighbourhoods hidden deep in the hills were being rapidly developed. This area is referred to as uptown and includes the neighbourhoods of La Dehesa, Lo Barnechea and Santa María de Manquehue. It is sometimes jokingly referred to as 'the United States' because the houses, stores and layout resemble those of any neighbourhood in California. Other affluent neighbourhoods are Las Condes, Los Dominicos, El Golf, Vitacura and parts of Providencia. The subway, or Metro, does not yet reach into the majority of the upscale areas, so living among the wealthy requires a car.

Foreigners also live in the middle-class districts of Providencia, La Reina, Ñuñoa and parts of the municipality of Santiago, such as downtown, Parque Forestal or República Street. There are some beautiful old houses and modern apartment buildings in these municipalities. They are also better served by public transportation and located nearer to supermarkets and other stores.

It is important to keep in mind that people move to Chile under many different circumstances. Students and people new to the workforce will experience a different side of Chile from those upper level employees sent by their firms with hefty incentive packages. For the latter, most likely you will live in the most affluent parts of town, and although you may consider yourself middle-class in your home country, in Chile you will live like the wealthy. Do not believe that the majority of Chileans have access to all the creature comforts that you do, like a spacious house, central heating and private schools. Other expats who move to Chile on their own, may not enjoy the benefits a large international firm provides, but will get to know Chile on a more intimate level, living as the majority of Chileans do.

CLIMATE

Due to the fact that Chile is in the southern hemisphere, the seasons are reversed from those in the northern hemisphere. Winter begins in April and September signals the advent of spring. The first of November is a public holiday that marks the unofficial beginning of summer. Schools have summer vacation from Christmas until the end of February. Many offices close for vacation in February. If you arrive in Chile in January or February, it will be very difficult to locate people. Everyone returns to their regular schedule in March as the temperatures begin to drop and classes resume.

The central region, where Santiago is located, has a Mediterranean climate. Spring and fall are mild and quite pleasant. Winters are cold and damp. Santiago has an average annual rainfall of about 355 mm (14 inches), most of which occurs between April and September. Temperatures drop down to 3°C (37.4°F), leaving you with a chill that cannot be shaken. In summer, temperatures can soar to 34°C (93°F) or higher. However, it is a very dry heat that is not altogether uncomfortable. Summer evenings are cool and refreshing. You will notice the lush lawns and overflowing window boxes in the residential areas of Santiago. Yet because the summer is so dry, it is only with constant watering that these beautiful gardens stay alive.

In northern Chile the weather remains mild all year long. Temperatures average 27°C (80.6 F) in summer and 14°C (57°F) in winter. In the Lake District, it rains most of the year and never gets really hot in the summer, although there are pronounced seasons. Average temperatures in the summer months hover around 20°C (68°F) and fall to 4°C (39.2°F) in the winter. Temperatures in the extreme south drop below freezing and strong winds make it feel even colder. The south receives over 2,300 mm (90 inches) of rain a year, and the islands of western Patagonia receive over 4,100 mm (160 inches) of rain a year!

TIME ZONE
Chilean time is four hours behind Greenwich Mean Time during mid-March to October (daylight savings time during the winter) and is three hours behind for the remainder of the year. Because of Chile's elongated shape, the entire country is in the same time zone.

POLLUTION
The major health concern in Santiago is air pollution. Although emission levels are relatively similar to the ones encountered in other large cities, geography makes pollution a serious problem. Santiago lies in a valley between two mountain ranges. This causes the contaminants to become trapped over the city. Everyday a thick layer of smog hangs over the downtown area and slowly travels eastward to the affluent neighbourhoods at the base of the mountains. For this reason it is said to be 'democratic' pollution.

The smog is responsible for a high incidence of respiratory diseases and premature deaths. The situation is worse in winter when children and older citizens are severely affected. Rain is the only effective manner of ridding the city of the smog. Following a downpour, the sky is clear and the snow-

capped mountains sparkle in the sunlight. It is an amazing sight and one is always taken aback by the fact that these huge mountains are so close, yet virtually blocked from view.

Exercise Indoors

For those who enjoy working out, it is healthier to do so indoors due to Santiago's notorious smog. When Susan's office moved she opted to walk to work, only 10 minutes away. Within three days she came down with a terrible cold from the pollution and decided that it was in her best interest to take the Metro two stops. White shirts and blouses turn grimy very quickly. Those who can, leave the city on weekends. Once out of Santiago the air is clean and fresh, especially along the coast.

Anti-Pollution Measures

You may be surprised to learn that the situation is much better than it was during the 1980s! The government has instituted a number of pollution fighting measures. The increased use of alternative energy and the closing of factories within the metropolitan area have helped. Vehicle emissions, however, remain a serious problem.

Restricción is a government imposed system which restricts the use of vehicles in an attempt to reduce pollution levels. It

Although not scientifically proven, there is a saying in Chile that goes: 'A ring around the moon, nothing will occur. A ring around the sun, a tempest or earthquake will certainly come.'

covers all vehicles without catalytic converters and is in effect Monday through Friday with the exception of public holidays. Each day of the week is assigned two numbers. Any personal vehicle whose license plate ends with either of the two numbers is not allowed to drive within the Santiago metropolitan region from 7:30 am until 9:00 pm. When particles in the air surpass the 100 microgrammes per cubic metre level, the government calls an Alert. At this time, four numbers are restricted from driving on that day. When levels surpass the 300 level, the government declares a Pre-emergency. On these days, six numbers are listed and cars without catalytic converters whose license plates end in those numbers are barred from driving. In addition, two numbers are listed for cars with catalytic

converters, and those cars are prohibited from driving as well. These numbers are clearly advertised in newspapers and on television and the policy is enforced. Drivers caught breaking the law must pay a hefty fine. Commercial vehicles and factories are also subject to restriction, under a different set of guidelines.

Although vehicle exhaust and emissions from nearby factories are the major contributors to smog, dust is another serious culprit. Santiago is a very dry and dusty city and studies have recommended paving more roads to address the pollution problem. However, critics argue that that would only serve to raise temperatures within the city.

LITTER

You may be shocked by the amount of litter thoughtlessly strewn about, especially in common public areas and along highways. Driving along the road you will undoubtedly see people toss garbage from car or bus windows. Although Chileans keep their homes and private areas neat and tidy, sadly there is a lack of understanding that common areas are their responsibility too. This can be blamed partly on successive governments that have failed to institute anti-littering campaigns. Chileans are under the impression that it is solely the government's responsibility to clean up and maintain public areas. Municipalities hire labourers to sweep up the plazas, sidewalks and streets, but clearly this is not enough. Graffiti and political propaganda can also be seen everywhere.

EARTHQUAKES

Tremors in Chile are quite common and if you do not come from an area prone to earthquakes it will be a frightening adjustment. Over the years, Chile has been struck by several earthquakes with a force greater than 6.9 on the Richter scale. The city of Valparaíso has been demolished on half a dozen occasions. In 1960 quakes struck southern Chile and caused giant tidal waves that swept inland and killed thousands of people. Central Chile shook in March of 1985, killing more than 100 people and leaving thousands homeless.

If one strikes, the best advice is to brace yourself in a door frame. Always leave shoes or slippers next to your bed while sleeping in case the floor becomes covered with broken glass. If you are in the city, do not run outside as there is a danger of being hit by falling electrical lines. Buildings in urban areas are built according to earthquake resistant codes. In rural areas where houses may be less resilient and power lines far away, it is best to be outside. It is always good to have bottled water on hand in case water mains are ruptured and contaminated. Also, when decorating your home take care to secure fragile items so that they do not easily fall during a tremor. Chances are you will not experience a major earthquake (*terremoto*) during your stay, but you will notice the minor tremors (*temblor*).

POISONOUS SPIDERS

There are two poisonous spiders in Chile, the araña del trigo, generally found in wheat fields, and the araña de rincón. You may want to buy a guidebook to help identify these species.

HOUSEHOLD ISSUES
House vs. Apartment
The first decision that you must make is whether to live in a house or an apartment. Many well-off Chileans prefer to live in apartment buildings because of the security they provide. Houses, in spite of the tall gates and alarm services, are more susceptible to break-ins. For those only staying in Chile for a short time, there is a good supply of furnished apartments (*departamentos amoblados*) or apart hotels. Real estate and relocation agencies can help you figure out what best suits your needs.

Long-term apartment leases are normally signed on an annual basis, renewable with two months notice. A deposit equivalent to one or two months rent is customary. If a real estate agent is involved, you will have to pay him or her the equivalent of half of one month's rent for services. The landlord will normally also pay the real estate agent a similar amount.

Renters are responsible for paying *gastos comunes* (condo fees). These are paid directly to the building management on a monthly basis and are separate from rent, which is paid to the owner. This fee covers maintenance of the building, i.e., elevators, lights, etc. and pays the salaries of the building employees. In general, the more expensive your apartment, the higher the *gastos communes* will be. It is computed in relation to the size of your apartment and may run anywhere from US$ 30 to US$ 200 and above depending on the services your building provides. When apartment hunting, be sure to ask the amount of *gastos communes* to avoid any unpleasant budgetary surprises later on. Also, make sure that there is no extra fee for the parking space. High-end housing most often comes with kitchen appliances, but moderate housing generally does not. This means that you will have to purchase your own stove, refrigerator, microwave, light fixtures, etc.

Estufas

One appliance you may not be familiar with is the *estufa* (space heater). Many pricey new houses and apartments are now equipped with central heating, although it tends to be very expensive. More moderately priced and older housing does not have central heating. Santiago experiences

an uncomfortable damp cold in the winter which makes an *estufa* a must for every major room in the house. Because most Chileans have only two or three *estufas*, some rooms are closed off for the winter.

There are three types of *estufas*: gas, electric and kerosene (*parafina*). Kerosene is the older and cheaper type, and tends to be the most popular. Once the wick is lit, it glows red for hours. Kerosene can be purchased at most gas stations (buy your own reusable container). Because the kerosene gives off an unpleasant smell, many people put a bowl of water with eucalyptus leaves or orange rinds on top of the heater. It should never be used in a small room and doors to other rooms need to be left open a crack for air circulation. When extinguishing the flame, major fumes are emitted by the *estufa*. Therefore, they should only be extinguished in a well ventilated, preferably outdoor area.

Electric *estufas* are an expensive way to heat a room because they are not very efficient. However, they are the easiest, cleanest and most convenient to use. It is tempting to purchase an electric *estufa* because all you need to do is plug it in, but be prepared for a very high electric bill.

Gas *estufas* are cheaper than electric *estufas* and more convenient than kerosene *estufas*. Some use gas that is piped into your home directly, but most use refillable gas canisters. Arrangements can be made with any of a number of companies that will pick up the old gas canisters and deliver new ones when needed. Or, you can purchase a new canister from a truck that passes up and down the streets. The workers bang the canisters to alert you of their arrival. The gas *estufa*, like the kerosene *estufa*, also works by using an open flame, but it gives off no fumes and can be extinguished inside. Catalytic *estufas* use cleaner gas as fuel and are healthier and safer, but more expensive.

Estufas are safe if used properly. Extra special care should be taken if you have small children. *Estufas* should not be used in bathrooms, left unattended or placed near anything flammable, like curtains, and they must be turned off before going to bed. Some mornings may be unbearable, but that is part of the charm of living in Chile.

Along with *estufas*, fireplaces are making a comeback, with newer, cleaner designs. Old style fireplaces cannot be used in Santiago in winter, in observance of anti-pollution laws. *Salamandras*, or cast-iron wood burning heaters, are also very common.

Chileans often complain about the cold and you will repeatedly hear the term *friolento* (a person who becomes cold quite easily). Make sure that you have plenty of blankets, long underwear and turtlenecks to prepare for winter. Residents of northern Wisconsin, Chicago and even Moscow have complained that the coldest winter they've ever experienced was the one they spent in Santiago.

Califont

The *califont* is the gas water heater that is generally located in the kitchen or bathroom. Many Chileans turn on the *califont* and light the pilot light every time they wish to use hot water, preferring not to leave it on when not in use. Old *califonts* should probably continue to be completely turned off when no longer needed for safety reasons. When you turn on the hot water do not be surprised by the loud whooshing noise it makes as it ignites to heat the water. Getting the right water temperature can be somewhat tricky and if the appliance is old, the temperature can change suddenly, making showers more interesting. If you have the option, a newer model is preferred because older *califonts* are prone to gas leaks and ventilation problems.

Utilities and Internet

Utilities are very efficient and function regularly with minor disturbances, if any. Most houses come with a phone line, or you can get one through the phone company (e.g. Telefónica). There are several competing long distance providers, as well as internet providers. Dial-up Internet access is cheap or free, but be careful with the phone charges. There are also several cellular phone providers. Some companies bundle services (cable TV, telephone and broad-band Internet service).

Utility companies require identification (I.D. card or passport) and proof of residence to open an account and

begin service. Most utilities can be requested by phone or via the Internet. Only under special circumstances would you need to go to their offices to order them in person.

Water is potable. Susan drank water directly from the tap and never had any health problems. Most people arriving in a new country will have minor stomach upsets as they become accustomed to the change in overall diet and water. If you are in Chile for a long period of time, you could sign up for a bottled water service or you may just want to risk an initial bout of 'chilenitis'. There are no long lasting implications and after an episode you should become immune to some of the common bacteria. However, if diarrhoea persists you should see a doctor.

Public Toilets

Upscale restaurants and shops provide clean and modern restrooms. However, more modest businesses may not have toilet paper and it is always a good idea to carry your own supply. Sewer systems in some older buildings and houses, especially in rural areas where septic tanks are used, cannot

adequately process toilet paper. In these places, used toilet paper should be thrown away not flushed. If there is no wastebasket right next to the toilet, it is a sign that toilet paper can in fact be flushed.

Maids

Many middle-class and upper-class families have maids (*empleadas*) or nannies (*nanas*). Most Chileans use the terms interchangeably, but technically nannies take care of the children in addition to doing the housework. In the past, most maids lived with the family, but today the number is split between live-in (*puertas adentro*) maids and those who come only for the day (*puertas afuera*). Most maids are expected to clean, cook, do laundry, iron and take care of the children. They wear their own clothes. If you would like them to wear a uniform, you are expected to provide it. You should at least provide them with a *delantal* (housecoat) to wear over and protect their clothes. Live-in maids do not work on Sundays. The current salary for a full-time live-in maid is about US$ 250 per month.

A lot of these women come from low-income backgrounds and a large percentage come from the Temuco area and are of Indian origin. Peruvian maids working illegally in Chile are becoming a common addition to Chilean households.

Maids who work on a daily basis often have their own families and live in lower-income neighbourhoods. A maid who has been with the same family for a very long time is practically considered a member of that family and is treated well.

Families who are searching for a maid use the '*nana* network'. Most maids have a friend or a relative who is looking for work with a family. If you are looking to hire a maid you can either ask around or go to an agency. The agencies may provide more guarantees, but regardless of how the maid is hired, you would be well advised to insist on talking to her former employers. Although most are trustworthy, there are always a few bad apples. You may want to keep a copy of her *Carnet de Identidad*. Finally, if you go on vacation ask her to return the keys. You may find your maid to be loyal and trustworthy, but you can never be sure who has access to her keys.

Laws protecting maids state, among other things, that in addition to salary, an employer must contribute to the employee's retirement fund and health care plan. Working hours, breaks and days off are also dictated by law. The government makes every attempt to ensure that these laws are observed and if a maid can prove non-compliance, her employer faces stiff financial penalties. Although a significant number of people circumvent the law, either by arrangement with the maid (i.e., she receives a higher salary but no contributions to health care) or because she is unaware of her rights, you should make sure you follow the local laws. For more details contact the Ministry of Labour.

Repairmen

Depending upon the rental agreement, you may be responsible for repairs in your home. Most likely, the landlord will handle major repairs, but you will have to take charge of minor problems. There are two options for finding a repairman (*maestro*). First, the telephone book has a long list of professional services under *reparaciones*. If the problem concerns electricity or gas, the best suggestion is to call the company or a professional service.

For other minor repairs, however, a cheaper alternative is to ask the *mayordomo* (superintendent) or *conserje* (superintendent) of the building if you live in an apartment or your maid if they know anyone who can do the job. Most likely they can provide you with the name of a *maestro* who can fix 'anything'. It is important to ask someone you trust, because some *maestros* are much better than others, in terms of both ability and punctuality. Make sure you stress exactly what you want done, otherwise it may turn into a bigger project than desired. A common practice is for the *maestro* to come first to look at the problem and ask for money in advance to buy parts. He will set up a time to return to complete the project. Rarely will someone take the money and not do the job, especially if he was recommended by a friend. Also, using a false ID from a professional service to gain access to your house is not a common crime in Chile. Most *maestros* are trustworthy, but you should never leave them alone in your home. A professional service can be paid by cash or check and you may tip the repairman. If you hire someone from a small shop or an independent *maestro* no tip is necessary.

Most people who own or rent a home in Santiago hire a gardener (*jardinero*) to take care of the yard. If you rent, most likely the gardener hired by the previous occupants will continue to work for you (although there is no written contract). However, you are required to pay for his services (not the landlord). Of course, if you are not happy with the service, you are free to hire someone else. This is also true of swimming pool maintenance companies, except that there is usually a formal contract between the parties. Often, gardeners and handymen will ring your doorbell soliciting their services.

Mail
If you live in a house, or even in some apartment buildings, mail carriers deliver mail to you directly. Technically, the carrier should be paid a small amount (a few pesos) for each piece of mail that is delivered. Most people pay a lump sum at the end of each month.

If you are having a large package sent from abroad, it will go through customs and once cleared, a notice will be sent to your address. The recipient must go to customs to pick it up in person, with a form of identification. If items can be sent separately in legal-size envelopes, they will not get stuck in customs and will be delivered right to your door.

Garbage and Cartoneros

If you live in a house, refuse should be placed outside your home the night before garbage collection. It is a good idea to place it up high (some people hang it from trees or use handy purpose built stands) to prevent stray dogs from shredding the bags and scattering litter all over the street. Also, you may hear, late at night, someone rummaging through your garbage. *Cartoneros* ride around the streets on their bicycle carts scavenging for anything that can be sold or recycled such as cardboard, glass, paper, etc. You may want to leave these items out separately to save them from having to go through the garbage.

MEDICAL SERVICES

The quality of health care depends upon whether the facilities are private or public. Private hospitals and clinics provide excellent care, modern facilities and high-tech equipment. You should have no trouble finding a doctor who speaks English, French, German, Italian, etc. Call your embassy for all the relevant information. The most highly respected hospitals are Clínica Las Condes, Clínica Alemana and Clínica Vitacura.

In case of a medical emergency, most Chileans call the police first (dial 133) because they respond immediately. There is a direct number to request an ambulance listed on the front page of the phone book, but the police can also have one sent to you. Over the past few years private emergency services have emerged. Members pay a monthly fee and are registered with the service. Non-members may also call and request help, although the fee will be higher. These services began with heart patients, but have spread to include other medical conditions and accidents. Some services also have contracts with individual schools and corporations.

Pharmacies in Chile sell medicine and toiletries. Large supermarkets normally have a pharmacy on site. Many drugs can be bought over the counter without a prescription. In fact, if you're not feeling well you can discuss the symptoms with the pharmacist, who will suggest appropriate medications. Select pharmacies are open 24 hours for emergencies.

DOCUMENTATION
Visas

If you plan on going to Chile as a tourist, a tourist visa good for 90 days (note: not 3 months) will be required. Residents of some countries, due to reciprocity, are limited to shorter stays. Depending on your citizenship, this will either be issued by a Chilean consulate or by immigration upon arrival. Upon entering Chile you will need to show a passport and sometimes a return travel ticket or ticket to a third country. (Citizens from Argentina, Brazil, Colombia, Paraguay and Uruguay need only have an identity card.) You will also need to fill out a tourist card. Hold on to your copy as this needs to be returned when you leave the country. Not having the tourist card will cause a huge hassle and delays as you try to catch your plane. Citizens of Canada, Australia, Mexico and the United States must pay a reciprocity fee either in cash or by credit card when they arrive at the Santiago Airport. US citizens must pay the highest amount, a whopping US$ 100. You must pay only once for the life of your passport. After immigration, travellers pass through customs. The following items are prohibited and will be confiscated: fruit, vegetables, seeds, non-processed animal products, illegal drugs, firearms and explosives.

If you are planning a longer stay in Chile, you will need either a work, student or temporary resident visa. A number of documents are required. For specific information call the nearest Chilean consulate or visit their website. Chile has embassies and consulates throughout the Americas, in most European countries, in several Asian countries and in a few African counties.

DOCUMENTATION NEEDED FOR VISAS

For Student Visa

- acceptance letter from school
- proof of loans, scholarship or ability to pay
- passport
- medical report, including HIV test
- police report
- four passport photos

For Contract (work) Visa

- passport
- medical report, including HIV test
- police report
- four passport photos
- letter explaining reason for visa
- Your employer needs to present the contract and request a visa in Santiago

For Temporary Residence Visa

- passport
- medical report, including HIV test
- police report
- four passport photos
- proof of relation to a Chilean citizen or permanent resident
- letter explaining reason for visa

Carnet

Each Chilean has an identification card called a *Carnet* or *Cédula de Identidad* bearing a RUN (*Rol Unico Nacional*) number, which is a number assigned to each person at birth. This number is used for all official documents, i.e., *carnet*, passport, taxpayer ID number, driver's license and voter ID card. Chileans commonly refer to this number as their *carnet* number, not their RUN. A RUT is a taxpayer ID number that is granted to individuals and corporations, both local and foreign, who are conducting business in Chile and must pay taxes.

After you have received your visa, you will be issued a *Carnet de Identidad* with an ID number and you will be requested to register with a special section of the police that deals with immigration, called *Policía Internacional*. You will be asked to provide your carnet number on numerous occasions, so memorise it or always have it on hand.

Getting a Driver's License

Many foreigners drive in Chile with a driver's license from their home country. Technically, an international driver's license should be obtained in the home country before leaving. Foreigners who expect to be in Chile for a long period of time should apply for a Chilean driver's license. This can be done at the office of the municipality in which you reside. You will need to present your *Carnet de Identidad* and take three tests: a written test in Spanish, a road test and a medical exam that checks vision, hearing and reflexes.

BANKING

Currency

The Chilean currency is the peso and if you're used to dollars or Euros, you'll have to get used to thinking in large numbers. Coins come in denominations of 1 peso (worth very little and very rarely used), 5 pesos, 10 pesos, 50 pesos, 100 pesos and 500 pesos. Bills are issued in 500; 1,000; 2,000; 5,000; 10,000; and 20,000 peso denominations. In Chilean slang, 1 *luca* is equivalent to 1,000 pesos and 1 *guatón* (fat one) is equal to 1 million pesos. A Gabriela is a 5,000 peso bill (graced by the portrait of poet Gabriela Mistral). If you are buying a cheap item, small bills and coins are appreciated, especially in the markets and in rural areas.

US dollars are not widely accepted, so you will have to change money upon arrival. It is customary for travellers cheques to trade at a slightly lower rate than cash. You will need to go to a *casa de cambio* as many banks do not perform this service. If provided, the bank will always offer a lower exchange rate than the *casa de cambio*. For a fee, the *casa de cambio* will also issue or cash a cheque in US dollars. There are a number of *casas de cambio* along Agustinas Street between Morandé Street and Estado Street downtown and on Pedro de Valdivia Avenue, just north of Providencia

Avenue in the Providencia district. You will undoubtedly be approached by hawkers whispering "*Dólares*" as you walk down Agustinas Street. They do not offer better rates than the *casas de cambio* and are not trustworthy. One American who worked on Wall Street was cheated by one of these guys who had rigged his calculator. Due to the number of zeros involved, you can get confused quite easily. Also, do remember to be careful upon leaving a *casa de cambio*. Experienced pickpockets prey on Chileans and foreigners alike, exiting *casas de cambio* and banks. *Casas de cambio* usually close for two hours for lunch around 2:00 pm.

Chilean banks offer an array of services including checking accounts, ATMs (*cajero automático*), savings accounts, credit cards, on-line bill payment, mutual funds, and *redcompra* (a debit card system). Banks each have their own forms that must be filled out, but all require a RUN number. Banks open at 9:00 am and close for the day at 2:00 pm on weekdays and do not open at all on Saturdays or Sundays. ATMs are abundant, but many charge fees and limit withdrawals to US$ 400 per day.

Bills

Chileans like to pay their utility bills in person. Each bill lists payment locations on the reverse side. Payment can usually be made at a specific bank, supermarket, payment centre or utility office. Payment can be made either by cheque or in cash. You can also instruct your bank to deduct utility charges directly from your current account. Paying on-line has caught on in Chile, making bill paying much more convenient. Payment by mail is rare.

Cheques and Credit Cards

Many Chileans make all purchases with a cheque. Laws against writing bad cheques are very strict and it is considered a serious offence. Therefore, cheques are accepted everywhere, i.e., stores, restaurants, gas stations, etc., provided that you show your *carnet* or passport. People normally write their *carnet* and telephone number on the back of the cheques they issue, to facilitate the transaction.

A *cheque cruzado* (showing two parallel lines drawn on the front) cannot be cashed, it can only be deposited. A *cheque a fecha* is a cheque with a future date. There is no obligation to wait until then to cash it or deposit it, but the system is generally honoured so these cheques can be used as credit or as collateral. A *cheque al día* has the current date so that it can be immediately cashed or deposited. Crossing out the words *al portado*r (to the bearer) printed on the front of cheques, makes it a *cheque nominativo*, that is, only the original bearer can cash it. A *chirimoyo* is slang for a bad cheque.

Credit cards are widely accepted, although your *carnet* or passport number will be requested. Debit cards are also widely used.

EMERGENCIES
Crime
Crime in Santiago is similar to that in any other major city. Pickpockets are a problem, particularly in the downtown area, especially if you look like an easy target, i.e., a lost tourist. You should not stroll through downtown after dark, particularly near the Plaza de Armas, which can become quite seedy at night. Being alert and knowing where you are can help you protect yourself. A few years back, the municipality of Santiago installed overhead police cameras in the downtown area in order to deter crime. Their presence, along with other measures, has helped reduce crime in this zone by 20 per cent. Another area that should be avoided at night is the Santa Lucia Hill. With all its nooks and crannies, it is an ideal location for muggings. Even during the day, women should not visit this park alone. The park is perfectly safe if you go as part of a group and the view from the top of the hill is well worth the steep climb.

Chile has a low murder rate, much lower than that of other Latin American and North American cities. While Chile remains a relatively safe country, there has been a steady increase in property crimes in Santiago. Poorer neighbourhoods (with higher rates of unemployment and drug abuse) tend to have higher crime rates, but the number of home invasions in wealthy areas is increasing. Most houses and some new apartments come with a security system. Yet, chances are small that you will be the victim of a crime during your stay.

The Police

The police in Chile are called the *Carabineros*. In any type of emergency the best advice is to call them first at 133. They will respond quickly and direct your call to any other agency needed, such as the fire department or an ambulance service. Bribes are not common practice in Chile and under no circumstances should you attempt to bribe a *Carabinero*. This will only get you into trouble. Chileans refer to the police as *pacos*, and although not an insult, the slang term is not preferred by the police themselves. The other branch of the Chilean police force is called *Policía de Investigaciones* (Investigations Unit). These are the plain-clothed police, or detectives.

Fire Department

You may often see *bomberos*, as firemen are called, out collecting donations in the streets. This is because all firemen in Chile are volunteers, with the exception of paid professional fire departments at the airport, in the armed forces and in certain industries. *Bomberos* are highly respected in Chile and some units are more prestigious than others. Many units are comprised of members from certain ethnic groups (the French Company, for example) or from certain professions (i.e., lawyers). All volunteers undergo rigourous training and there is a strict hierarchical order within each company. Although they are not paid a salary, fire fighters receive other forms of compensation, for example, meals or shelter. Fire departments are funded by the State, by members' contributions, by public donations and by revenue from lotteries that by law must contribute a certain portion to charities, etc. However, most units run on very tight budgets, so feel free to donate!

Firefighters in Chile are volunteers and many companies are organised according to profession or ethnicity.

DRIVING

Driving in Santiago and along the Pan American Highway can be a harrowing experience. The number of cars on Chilean roads has increased dramatically over the past 15 years as Chileans have become more affluent. This sudden increase in new drivers combined with bad habits, poorly marked lanes and some questionable road signs can make driving in Santiago difficult. Once you are familiar with the city and with driving patterns commuting should get easier.

One of the biggest problems in Chile for foreigners is that cars share the road with pedestrians, old trucks, carts, bicycles and stray dogs. Vendors dash into the street trying to sell their wares to motorists. Once Susan even drove past a person in a wheelchair on a hill at night,

Most gas stations in Chile are still full service, so a small tip should be given to the gas station attendant.

with neither lights nor a reflector! In spite of the fact that the government has built a number of overpasses for pedestrians, most choose to dash across major highways instead. Moreover, the Pan American Highway runs through many small towns where it serves as the main thoroughfare.

Driving habits also may make you see red. It is not uncommon for a car to just stop on a busy street to pick someone up or let someone out, causing traffic to backup. Drivers also feel compelled to speed up and cut off other cars. They tend to veer from their lane, tailgate or turn from the wrong lane. A word of advice is to be prepared for anything.

Street vendors often ply their goods on busy street corners to motorists stopped in traffic.

By law, infants and toddlers need to be restrained in car seats in Chile. This law is seldom obeyed or enforced. You'll see children climbing over seats or hanging out the window while their parent drives. Parents still believe that they'll be able to hold on to a child held in their lap if there is an accident, or they may not want to disturb a sleeping baby by strapping it in. Susan met a woman who only used the car seat for long trips to the beach, but didn't want to be bothered with it in the city. This was the one topic of discussion among expat moms that brought out the most disbelief, anger and fear.

It is relatively easy to rent a car in any major city. Offices are located at airports, major hotels and downtown areas. A passport and valid driver's license from your own country or an international driver's license are required and most major credit cards are accepted.

If you plan on buying a car you can head to one of the dealers along Avenida las Condes or Avenida Bilbao. If you don't want to run all over town, you can go to a huge centre, such as Movicenter on Americo Vespucio, where various dealers share one large space. After you decide upon a car you should negotiate the final price. You should expect to pay about 10 per cent less than the sticker price.

Toll roads are becoming more common in Chile due to private investment in infrastructure. A few, like Costanera Norte in Santiago, will only accept electronic payment, so be alert.

Tickets

If you are pulled over by a *Carabinero* and given a ticket, your license will be taken away. You will be given the ticket and a summons to appear in court. You are allowed to drive on your ticket, unless the offence is very serious and your driving privileges have been revoked. In general, you must appear in the court of the municipality where the ticket was issued on the date specified, but you can pay the fine or ask for leniency through the *Juzgado de Policía Local* (Local Police Court) closest to your home. If you are found guilty a stiff penalty will be imposed. You cannot plead guilty

Bribery is not common practice in Chile and can incur strict penalties.

at the time of the offence and pay the policeman. Some municipalities implemented new procedures to simplify the process, whereby if you plead guilty you may pay the fine at a bank.

Cuidadores de Autos

Another common sight in Chile is the parking attendant, called a *cuidador de autos*. Many places where you park your car, be it on the street or in a private lot, within seconds a man or woman with a little handkerchief and/or flashlight will run over to your car to help guide you in. They aren't really paying attention, so don't rely on their assistance too much. Supposedly they watch the cars in their 'sector' while the owners are away to protect them from robberies. When leaving they once again help guide you out of your spot and it is customary to give them a small tip.

10 de Julio

Many auto repair shops in Santiago are concentrated on one street, 10 de Julio. In fact, on any given day this street is filled with mechanics fixing cars randomly parked off to the side. If the first shop doesn't have the necessary part, the mechanic will direct you to one further down the street. At the first sign of car trouble, head for 10 de Julio; just about anything you need can be found here and it can be a fun experience, if you value hands-on experience more than fancy auto-school titles. You can also take your car to a modern *autocentro* or to the dealership, but it is just not as interesting or cheap.

TRANSPORTATION
Metro

Santiago's Metro will eventually have five lines, which explains why the current lines are numbered 1, 2, 4 and 5. Line 3 is scheduled to be built later. Line 1 runs directly across the city from east to west: beginning in Maipú, passing through downtown, along Providencia up to Las

Metro is a safe, easy form of transportation in Santiago and is currently being expanded.

Condes. Plans have been made to expand this line farther up into Las Condes. Lines 2, 4 and 5 run perpendicular to Line 1 and serve heavily populated middle-class and lower middle-class neighbourhoods. Service is efficient, but during rush hour (8:00–9:30 am and 6:00–7:30 pm) demand exceeds space and the cars are very crowded. It is best to force your way to the door before you arrive at your station, as it is not the custom for those blocking the doors to step off and let you exit.

Buses

Buses in Chile are called micros and smaller buses are called *liebres* (hares). The new Transantiago bus system was recently introduced in Santiago. This system coordinates all of the buses with the Metro and utilises electronic fare payment and smart cards. Most buses are brand new and environmentally friendly. Transantiago had a rocky start but should improve with time.

Figuring out which bus you need to take can be somewhat tricky at first and the ride can be a jolting experience. Signs are posted in the front window of every bus listing all the streets on its route. Therefore, the trick is to know major streets before and after your desired stop. The other option is to ask the driver if he goes where you are going, which is a very common practice. (*Pasa po*r x street or landmark?) Once you become familiar with the geography of Santiago it will be much easier and you'll be hopping on and off buses like any Santiaguino. For routes and schedules, check out http://www.transantiago.cl

The bus ride itself may prove interesting. Throughout Chile, hawkers often board the bus selling ice cream, candy, pencils, etc. (They request permission from the bus driver first and do not pay.) Others may board with guitars or other musical instruments and play and/or sing. Prior to the performance many may tell you a sob story about how they are former prisoners trying to stay on the right side of the law. Most likely a few are telling the truth, but some use it as a ploy. Following the performance they will walk the length of the bus looking for tips. If you liked the performance, pay accordingly.

Occasionally a deaf person may board and distribute plastic cards with calendars or sayings to each passenger. Then, he goes back to collect the money. You are expected to return the card if you don't want to make a donation. However, with the implementation of Transantiago and its new rules, this may soon be a thing of the past. Bus rides in other cities may still prove interesting, though

Taxis

Taxis in Chile are black with yellow roofs and run on meters. In general, you should not negotiate a fixed price beforehand. There is an abundance of cabs and for the most part they are very safe. In Santiago, taxis are no longer allowed to enter a certain eight-block area in the centre without a passenger. Thus, if you are looking for a taxi and are within this radius you must find a taxi letting a passenger off. Of course, as a result of Chilean ingenuity, some cab drivers actually pay people to ride in the back of the taxi so that they can enter the zone in order to pick up higher fare passengers.

If it is late at night or you need a taxi to pick you up at someone's home you should call a radiotaxi. You must pay a small surcharge, but it is safe and prompt. Radiotaxi drivers will even run errands for you, like picking up medicines from the drugstore or make certain that children riding alone get home safely. Tourist taxis are commonly found at major hotels. The ride may be more luxurious, but the fare will be higher. Meters are not used in tourist taxis, so negotiate the price beforehand.

Airport Shuttles

When arriving at the airport in Santiago there are a number of options to get to the city, about a 30-minute drive away. Airport taxis are available and charge a fixed rate. A coupon must be purchased from the taxi counter beforehand. A cheaper alternative is a Transfer. This is a minivan that takes about four people to different destinations within the same part of Santiago. This service is provided by both the Chilean airlines and private companies. The ticket is also purchased at the company's counter located on the arrival level. You must tell them what part of Santiago you are going to and they will tell you which van to board. If you are the first to be dropped off, it's as quick as a taxi, if you are the last, it's about 15 minutes longer. The cheapest way to get into the city is to take an airport bus that will drop you off at either the Los Heroes Metro stop, or at a bus terminal downtown. If you need a ride to the airport all three forms of transportation are readily available in the opposite direction. Airport taxis are available at most large hotels. Any regular taxi will also take you to the airport, but some will most likely want to negotiate a fixed price beforehand. If you have a clear understanding of the value of Chilean currency you can negotiate a good price. The taxi drivers will try to make money, but will not try to rob you blind.

Colectivos

Colectivos look exactly like the black and yellow cabs but have a sign and number plate on top of the roof. These cars run predetermined routes and pick up as many passengers as will fit into the car. The cost is maybe double that of a bus, but far cheaper than a private taxi.

EDUCATION

Overall, Chile has a good education system. Not surprisingly, private schools have the best test scores. The government continues to reform the public school system. There are three types of schools—public or *pública* (government-funded and administered by the municipalities); private or *particular* (privately funded and run); and subsidised private or *particular subvencionada* (government-funded but privately administered). Many private schools were originally founded to serve an ethnic community or religious group. Some schools have two different locations, one for the primary school and another for the high school. Students in the same homeroom become very close as they study as one group for the entire eight or even 12 years.

In general, private schools provide the best education. However, this is not a hard and fast rule as there are a number of high quality public schools. Some upper-class

For years, students from neighbouring countries have come to Chile to receive a higher education. With the increase in the number of universities, there are now even greater opportunities for foreigners to study in Chile. Some universities provide tailored programmes for foreign students, so it is a good idea to shop around for the best programme.

private schools are extremely conservative and will not accept illegitimate children or children of parents who have separated. Public schools and subsidised private schools cannot exclude anyone because they receive government funding. If a foreign child is a legal resident of Chile (i.e., has a valid visa) he or she should not be legally barred from attending any school. Children whose parents are in the country illegally are never turned away from public schools either.

If your child does not speak Spanish, don't worry, there are a large number of private schools that offer instruction in a foreign language. When researching schools make sure you confirm whether classes are taught solely in the foreign language (plus a Spanish language class) or if it is a bilingual school where half of the classes are taught in the foreign language and the other half in Spanish. Also, certain institutions offer the foreign language only up to a certain grade level, when all instruction then switches over to Spanish.

There are so many foreign language schools all over Chile that they cannot be listed here. Some of the better known schools in Santiago are Nido de Aguilas (the American School), The Grange School, Craighouse, The Mayflower School, Santiago College, Southern Cross, St. Gabriel's School, St. George's College and Redland School. English language schools can be found in practically every other city in Chile. German and French schools can be found up and down the country and often rank among the best. You can also find Italian, Croatian and Hebrew schools. In general, foreign language schools have excellent reputations and consistently do well on standardised tests.

Documentation

To enrol your child in a Chilean school you will most likely be asked to fill out an application form, pay an application fee and provide an original birth certificate, a picture of the child and transcripts from previous schools. In some instances the child will have to take an exam and the parents will be interviewed. Once your child is accepted and you've decided on a school, you will have to pay a hefty registration fee for private, non-subsidised schools.

ENROLLING YOUR CHILD IN SCHOOL
Paperwork Needed
- application form
- original birth certificate
- transcripts from previous schools
- picture of child

Fees Payable
- application fee
- registration fee once child is accepted

Special Requirements
- exam
- parent interview

After School Activities
Children participate in many familiar after school activities, such as soccer, tennis, swimming, karate, basketball, volleyball, music lessons, etc. These may be offered through the school itself or through a sports clubs. Some of the most well-known clubs in Santiago are Club Deportivo Patricio Cornejo, Club Deportivo Universidad Católica, Universidad de Chile, and all of the *clubes de colonia* (national clubs) like the Estadios Italiano, Español, Croata, Israelita and Club Deportivo Manquehue (German).

Preschools
Preschools in Chile are called *jardines infantiles* and there are many different ones to chose from. There are several that operate in foreign languages, but you might want to consider putting your child in a Spanish-speaking preschool. This is a perfect age for your children to be immersed in another language. Children in preschool do not wear uniforms but

you will be expected to purchase from the school a *delantal* (smock) for them to wear everyday over their clothes.

Universities

The Chilean university system has a very good reputation, built primarily on the prominence of the two main traditional universities, Universidad Católica and Universidad de Chile. Degree programmes in medicine, law, engineering, economics, business (*ingeniero comercial*), agriculture and mining and marine sciences are among the best in the region. For this reason, many Latin Americans choose to study in Chile.

Prior to the 1980s, Chile had only a small number of traditional universities that received full or partial state funding. The military government decided to introduce competition into the system. Anyone who complied with certain requirements could open and run a university. 'New' universities are separate from the traditional universities, but are under their supervision until firmly established. Today there are over 30 new universities in Chile, a higher number than that of traditional universities. The traditional universities enjoy name recognition, are more prestigious and are assumed to have better professors. (It is common in Chile for practicing professionals to teach at the universities.) While the new universities are not considered to be diploma mills, they do not yet enjoy the same status as the traditional universities, with a couple of exceptions. In general, it is easier to be admitted into a new university, so there is an element of elitism for students and alumni of traditional universities.

University students in Chile enter a degree programme that takes roughly four to seven years to complete. Almost all classes pertain to the student's chosen field (*carrera*), unlike in some other countries where a wide range of topics is studied. Therefore, everyone studying the same subject knows each other but they do not have much interaction with students in other fields. In fact, different schools (the school of economics, the school of journalism, etc.) are located on various campuses, thereby segregating the students further. A *práctica* (internship) and a thesis are required of all students, most often during the final year of study.

Upon graduation, a *título* (degree) or a *licencia* (license) is conferred that allows the graduate to practice a specific profession. A person without this specific degree or license would not be able to work in the field. In this sense, it is very different from the system in the United States where students receive academic degrees that are quite flexible and allow the student to practice a wide range of professions. This difference explains the confusion surrounding questions about careers. In the United States, the question is "What do you do?" and the answer usually relates to one's current position, for example, "I'm a Marketing Director for (name of company)." In Chile, the question is "What are you?" and refers to your profession in general, not your specific job title. "I'm an economist, mathematician, an *ingeniero comercial*, a teacher, etc." If you have a more 'exotic' degree, such as in philosophy or international affairs, explaining what you are becomes a little more difficult, unless you have no problems claiming to be a philosopher or a global affairs pundit. Incidentally, in Chile—unlike most of Latin América—only physicians are referred to as doctors.

In order to apply to a university you must take the PSU (*Prueba de Selección Universitaria*). The PSU tests general knowledge of language, mathematics, history and science. Students don't take all parts of the test, only those related to their major. Admission requirements for the traditional universities are tough; applicants must have high test scores and a good high school record. There are a limited number of spaces, so competition is fierce. The requirements for private universities vary according to the school.

Spanish Programmes

Many Spanish-language programmes are offered in Chile. One of the best known in Santiago is the Instituto Chileno Norteamericano (North American-Chilean Institute). This institute, like several others, offers both Spanish and English courses, which promotes interaction between both groups. The Centro Chileno-Canadiense and the Goethe Institut also

Chile boasts large new shopping malls where almost anything can be found.

have good Spanish programmes, in addition to teaching English and German respectively. A number of universities and smaller institutes offer Spanish classes as well.

SHOPPING

Large, modern shopping malls and huge box stores are popping up everywhere in Chile, although many smaller stores still line the streets. Some of the major shopping malls in Santiago are Parque Arauco and Alto Las Condes, and new shopping centres can be found up in La Dehesa. The main department stores are Falabella, Almacenes París and Ripley. When making a purchase in a department store up to three different salespeople will wait on you. The person who makes the sale brings your purchase to the *caja* where you pay and get a stamped receipt. That salesperson then transfers your purchase to *empaque*. You present your receipt at *empaque* in order to pick up the wrapped goods.

Líder and Jumbo are cheaper big box stores that sell food, toiletries, clothing, and household items. Homecenter is the largest hardware store chain. These stores sell many goods imported from Europe, Latin America, the United States and Canada. The downtown area is full of *galerías*, large indoor networks of passageways lined with many small shops (ideal to avoid the rain and traffic!). Other areas that sell less expensive goods are Patronato Street and

What to Bring

Chile imports many items and you should be able to find just about everything you need. However, if you are very attached to a particular brand or item, you might want to bring it with you to be on the safe side. Books tend to be expensive and the selection of foreign language books is limited, so bring lots of reading material. Items associated with a holiday that is not celebrated in Chile should be brought as well. Many toilet articles and children's items tend to be a bit more expensive in Chile so you might want to stock up on them as well. Clothing in Chile may fit differently, requiring you to bring a full wardrobe from home. Finally, if you are taking a specific medication it may not be available in Chile. For electronics, remember that Chile runs 220 volts, not 110, so it may not be wise to bring these from home.

the outlet mall in Maipú. *Mercados persas* or just *persas* are permanent flea markets/bazaars. Each *persa* is made up of a number of small stalls selling almost anything at very low prices. Two of the biggest *persas* are Persa Bío-Bío (in the *comuna* of Santiago) and Persa Estación by the Estación Central train station. Also, there are a lot of very cheap used clothing stores in Providencia and downtown. Most of the used clothing is imported from Europe. If you enjoy rummage stores, they are worth a peek for bargains or vintage items. Except for the malls, all stores close Saturday at 2:00 pm and are closed all day Sunday.

Clothing

In Chile, prices for high-quality items, especially clothes and imported toiletries can be quite steep. There is, of course, a wide range of cheaper items of lower quality. Clothing tends to run smaller than in the United States so large men and women may have a problem finding clothes in their size. The clothing also tends to be cut for the Mediterranean woman's figure. Some women may find it doesn't fit properly in the hips and waist. Ask about a good *modista* (seamstress) for tailor-made outfits. In fact, because well-made ready-to-wear clothing can be quite expensive and labour costs are still quite low, having clothes made by a tailor is a good option for men's clothing as well. Women's shoes also run small, usually up to a US size 8 or European size 38. Chile has a successful shoe industry, in addition to cheap imports from Brazil and China, so you will find a wide selection of footwear at reasonable prices. Finally, because it is difficult to return items once purchased, make sure you buy the right size and that you like it.

Dress

Older women continue to wear skirts, although younger Chilean women are now heavily influenced by fashion trends in the United States and Europe. Previously, shorts were worn only at the beach, but you will now see them all over Santiago during the summer. It is advisable not to bring white clothing, as it gets dirty very quickly due to the pollution and dust. For this same reason, shoes tend to suffer from more wear and tear than elsewhere.

For those whose residence does not have central heating, winters mean low temperatures indoors. You must bundle up during the winter and heavy sweaters, turtlenecks and scarves are a good idea. Men often wear sweater vests under their suitcoats.

School Clothes

Practically all schoolchildren are required to wear uniforms, whether in public or private schools. University students are expected to dress nicely for class. Most wear trendy casual clothes and jeans are acceptable, but ratty T-shirts and shorts are not appropriate. Hats are never worn indoors and shoes are never removed during class. The professor has the right to ask you to leave if he finds your dress unacceptable.

Practically all students in Chile wear uniforms to school, whether public or private.

Crafts

Undoubtedly, you will want to buy souvenirs for family and friends as well as yourself. Typical Chilean products and crafts include Lapis Lázuli, copper items, pottery, pewter and silver. The Bellavista neighbourhood is filed with stores that stretch up Avenida Santa María. *Ferias* are markets or fairs where you can find Chilean crafts. Some popular ones are Feria Santa Lucía across from Santa Lucía Hill, Pueblo de Artesanos de Los Dominicos at the end of Avenida Apoquindo, El Faro on Avenida Manquehue and La Aldea de Vitacura on Vitacura Avenue. These are great places to buy souvenirs for friends and family back home. These vendors tend not to offer huge discounts but at *ferias* outside of Santiago, you should be able to negotiate a better price.

The Informal Sector

The informal sector plays an important part in the country's economy. People sell candy, ice cream, fruit, toys, etc. on buses and on street corners, walking up and down the street when traffic is stopped at a red light. Vendors can be seen with their wares laid out on a blanket on the sidewalk, ready to fold it up and disappear when the police show up. You can buy almost anything on the street, from jewellery and accessories to pirated music and movies to dishtowels.

Chileans have full access to a free press. However, at times, it has been subject to censorship. A case involving La Tercera reflects the public's opposition to any kind of censorship. A drug-related case was being tried in Chile and some members of the judiciary had been implicated. The courts slapped a gag order on the Chilean press, preventing it from covering the trial. La Tercera set up a website in the United States in order to legally cover the trial. Unable to control the flow of information, the government relented and revoked the gag order.

STAYING INFORMED AND ENTERTAINED

If you can read and understand Spanish, the local media has very good news coverage. *El Mercurio*, the leading opinion-making newspaper, is very conservative and indirectly influenced by the church. It is considered a serious and traditional paper like *The New York Times* or *The Times* (London). The other prominent Santiago newspaper is *La Tercera*. This paper has been conservative in its treatment of topics like divorce and sex education. Nevertheless, *La Tercera* and another daily, *Las Ultimas Noticias*, are colourful and appeal to the masses. *La Nación* is a semi-official paper. *La Segunda* comes out in the afternoon and carries late-breaking news. It is common to hear the call of hawkers selling *La Segunda* in the downtown area in the afternoon. *La Cuarta* is a tabloid full of pictures of scantly clad women and hilariously written news. There are two very important financial papers, *El Diario Financiero* and *Estrategia*. Outside Santiago, every good-sized town has its own newspaper. Free newspapers, such as *La Hora*, are also widely available. There is a high concentration of media ownership, particularly printed media. All newspapers have good or excellent free websites. *El Mostrador* is an Internet only daily.

News Magazines

There are several news magazines published in Chile. *Ercilla* and *Qué Pasa* tend to sympathise with the right. *Cosas* and *Caras* both provide a peculiar mix of gossip and in-depth interviews with important people; for example you might find a story about European royalty next to a great interview with President Bachelet or the Dalai-Lama.

Foreign Language Media

The Santiago Times, part of CHIP (the Chilean Information Project) is an English language newspaper that covers issues important to Chile, including political, business and cultural topics. Their website is http://www.chipsites.com. *Chile News* is another English language paper, check out the website at http://www.newsreview.cl. *Business News America* (http://www.bnamericas.com) provides business news from Latin America on its website. *Chile Post* offers news related to Chile from a wide range of international sources on its website (http://www.chilejournal.com). There is a German language Chilean newspaper called *Wochenschau Chile der Zeitung CONDOR*. (http://www.condor.cl) A number of foreign language newspapers and magazines can be found at kiosks in the downtown area of Santiago.

Television

Cable and digital television in Chile is very good. You can receive Latin American, European and American channels in their original language for a fee. CNN has a Spanish language station in addition to its regular English broadcast. Chilean television offers a wide array of local programs, dubbed foreign language shows and movies. Reality and *farándula* (show-business gossip) programmes get huge audiences, as do music and dance shows.

Telenovelas

A cultural phenomenon common throughout Latin America is the soap opera or *telenovela*. Literally everyone watches the *telenovelas*. Foreigners are often shocked by how good they are, given the poor quality of such fare available in many other countries. Even Chilean men avidly watch them, and they are a topic of casual conversation among family members or good friends. Latin American *telenovelas* only last about five months, after which time they end and rarely have a sequel, allowing the actors to pursue other shows. The actors are household names in Latin America, and appear in many different *telenovelas*, so you will get to know them if you live in Chile for any length of time.

At first all the *telenovelas* will seem the same to you. But after a time you can distinguish the imports—from Mexico, Venezuela, Argentina and Brazil—from the local shows. If you are not well integrated into Chilean society it may be the best way for you to observe Chileans. However, as there is much talk and very little action, they may be hard to follow until your Spanish is very good. Chilean *telenovelas* are usually filmed in neighbourhoods around Santiago, places that you know. Chilean *telenovelas* have started to explore such modern topics as unwed mothers and AIDS.

Sábado Gigante

The Chilean television programme that has become an institution throughout the Americas is called *Sábado Gigante*, or Giant Saturday. As the name implies, it is long, and airs from 7:00 pm to 10:00 pm every Saturday on Univision.

A live audience participates in contests and watches skits, interviews, song and dance numbers and news reports. Don Francisco is the popular host of the show and has been on *Sábado Gigante* since its premier in Chile in 1962. His real name is Mario Kreutzberger, but everyone calls him by his stage name. Don Francisco hosts the version of the show that is taped in Miami, seen in practically every country in North and South America. His daughter Vivi hosts the Chilean version. Chileans are very proud of the fact that *Sábado Gigante* originated in Chile and is now the most widely watched show in all of Latin America. As Don Francisco says every week, "Latinos are *Separados por la distancia, unidos por el idioma.* (Separated by distance, united by language.)" One feels the sense of Latin American unity watching his programme.

Incidentally, Don Francisco is the force behind the annual Chilean *Teletón*, which every year collects millions of dollars for the rehabilitation of handicapped children. With massive corporate, media and people's support, *Teletón* genuinely brings the country together every December and is a source of strong national pride.

Cinema

Movies are popular in Chile, although the great majority are imported. Brand new theatres, complete with popcorn and multiple screens, make going to the movies a pleasant experience, even though Saturday nights can get very crowded. Movies are not dubbed (to the unending thanks of the expatriates), but subtitled, except for children's animated movies, where you can choose between dubbed and subtitled format. In Santiago you can find other original language films in Italian, German and French.

In older theatres seats are assigned in the cinema and you choose your seat when you buy the ticket. Tickets are half price on Wednesday. As a result, many shows are sold out, so if you want to take advantage of the bargain, buy your tickets either Tuesday or Wednesday morning. Many foreigners complain that the sound quality is not very good in the older theatres; perhaps because Chileans read the subtitles they do not mind.

Ballet, opera and classical music can be appreciated at the Teatro Municipal in downtown Santiago.

Renting movies in Chile is quite easy and video clubs are common. Most of the foreign movies can be watched in their original language. The Spanish movie title is not always a literal translation of the original title. We recommend you ask for films by actor if you are having problems locating a movie.

Radio

Chile enjoys a diverse radio programming spectrum, both in AM and FM bands. For many years, due to the fractured geography of the country, radio was the only way to reach everybody. Even today, radio shows featuring messages for families and individuals are common in the islands of Chiloé. You will be able to find your favourite music, both Latin and English-language pop, and will be able to hear news... but only in Spanish.

Theatre

For those who speak Spanish very well, there are plenty of good theatres. Teatro a Mil is a popular summer theatre festival in Santiago, featuring local and international companies. If your Spanish is not quite good enough for local theatre, Santiago Stage offers performances in English and the *Teatro Municipal* (Municipal Theatre) in downtown Santiago presents ballets, operas and classical concerts.

FOOD

CHAPTER 6

'In the storm-tossed Chilean sea lives the rosy conger,
giant eel of snowy flesh. And in Chilean stew pots
along the coast, was born the chowder,
thick and succulent and boon to man.'
—Pablo Neruda, *Oda al Caldillo de Congrio*

As EXPERIENCED EXPATRIATES, we know that food is one of the major components of culture shock. Three times a day, or perhaps even more, you are reminded that you are not in your homeland. Yet with any luck you will discover tasty Chilean delicacies that will be difficult to leave behind when your stay is over. Take advantage of your stay to collect Chilean recipes and try your hand at new and different meals.

SCHEDULE
Breakfast
The first meal of the day in Chile is *desayuno* or breakfast. It is rather light fare—bread with jam or butter and milk for the children and *café con leche* or tea for the adults. *Café con leche* is half a cup of hot coffee with half a cup of hot milk, sweetened to taste with sugar. Energy drinks such as Milo are also common for children.

Lunch
Almuerzo or lunch is the big meal of the day in Chile, and it is generally eaten between 1:00 and 2:00 pm. Traditionally, two main dishes are served at lunch. The first dish may be a salad of some kind. The second course is generally a more substantial meat, fish or pasta dish with vegetables as accompaniment, although there are several Chilean vegetarian main dishes. In small towns and in some parts of big cities, businesses close from 1:00 to 3:00 pm so

people can go home and have lunch with their families. Most businesses in the larger cities stay open all day.

Once

The third meal of the day, *once*, is at 5:00 pm, not 11:00 pm as the name implies. It is afternoon tea with bread and jam, sandwiches, pastries or a cake. It is very typical for children and adults alike to invite people over to share *once*.

A Teatime Tale

There are at least three versions of how teatime got its name in Chile. The first version claims that it is named after the time that the British have their tea—11:00 am. Another version claims that it is named after a variety of English biscuits called elevenses that the British served with their tea. The third version says that at teatime the men went to the kitchen or back room to have a sip of *aguardiente*, a grape spirit, instead of tea. However, the men didn't want to say that they were drinking liquor. Since the word *aguardiente* has 11 letters, they called it *once*.

Dinner

Dinner in Chile is referred to as *la comida* and not *cena* as in many other Spanish-speaking countries. Only in rural areas, particularly in the South, will you hear the word *cena*. Dinner is typically served at 8:00 pm if there are young children, or later if the children are older. If you venture into a restaurant before 9:00 pm you will find it quite empty. They only spring to life after this seemingly late hour so don't expect to eat dinner out at 5:30 pm if that is your normal routine. Normally, dinner is one main dish, which tends to be interchangeable with those served as a main course for lunch. The meal is substantial and foreigners may find it too heavy to eat at such a late hour.

MAIN COURSES
Seafood

As you can imagine, due to the geography of the country, there is an incredible variety of seafood available. Typical seafood dishes include: *choritos* (blue mussels), *pulpo* (octopus), *erizos* (sea urchin), *cochayuyo* (seaweed), *picorocos*, *centolla* (king crab), salmon, *machas* (clams), *locos* (abalone), *lenguado* (flounder), *merluza* (hake), *pejerrey* (smelt), *mero* (Chilean sea bass), *trucha* (trout), *congrio* (conger eel), *corvina* (white corvina), *ostras* (oysters) and *ostiones* (scallopes) just to name a few.

You can order your fish fillet *a la plancha* (grilled), *frito* (fried) or *poché* (poached) and if you like, it can be served with a sauce, such as *margarita* (a creamy sauce with crab and shrimps), *alcaparra* (caper sauce), *salsa verde* (hot pepper and parsley based) or *a la mantequilla* (with melted butter).

Seafood is served in soups and stew, in salads, *paella* (a Spanish rice dish), *chupe* (a casserole), on the grill or raw. *Ceviche*, raw seafood 'cooked' with lots of lemon juice, originated in Peru and is now popular in Chile. Another very popular dish is *locos* or abalone. Selling abalone out of season is illegal in Chile. The government has recently relaxed the restrictions as the population is making a comeback. Regardless, you might surreptitiously be offered some *locos* by a waiter.

Other Chilean novelties include *erizos* and *picorocos*. *Erizos* have a strong iodine flavour and are an acquired taste. *Picorocos* live in tube-like shells clustered together in colonies that resemble a rock. Their beaks stick out from the tubes. The Chilean way of eating them is to grab the beak, pull it out and swallow it raw. This delicacy is truly for the adventurous.

Beef

For a country that has such a long coastline, it is interesting that beef remains so popular. It is generally of good quality, but most Chileans admit that Argentinean beef is superior. There are a number of restaurants in Chile that serve only *parrilladas*. A *parrillada* is a small barbeque brought to your table overflowing with assorted cuts of beef and sausages. Some foreigners are shocked by *parrillada*, which can include almost every part of the beast, including intestines, stomachs, hearts and other tasty treats. They also include typical Chilean blood sausages, *prietas*. The name comes from the Portuguese word *preta* which means black. If these are not

to your taste be sure to request your preferred cuts or ask what it is before you accept it on your plate.

Another characteristic beef dish is *bistec a lo pobre*, a steak topped with two fried eggs and served with french fries and sauteed onions. Although the name means poor man's steak, Chileans joke that the name should be changed to *bistec a lo rico* (rich man's steak) since it is expensive. Do not confuse this typical meal with *steak au poivre*, which is a French pepper steak dish that is not common in Chile. *Carne mechada* is another popular dish. A thick piece of meat is tenderised in a vinegar marinade and cooked with carrots.

Special Dishes

Chileans have many main dishes where the principal ingredient is not meat or fish. One of the tastiest is *humitas*, made by grating fresh corn (*choclo*) and mixing it into a paste with fried onions, basil, salt and pepper. The mixture is then wrapped in cornhusks and dropped into boiling water to cook. The corn to make *humitas* has big individual kernels and is perfect for baking. Chilean corn is not sweet, like corn grown and eaten in the United States. Another typical Chilean main dish is *porotos granados*, a healthy combination of beans, squash and corn. Beans are called *porotos*, not *frijoles*, in Chile.

There is a common misperception that Chileans eat spicy food. Do not confuse the dishes of the Southern Cone with Mexican or Tex-Mex food. In general, the majority of Chilean meals are either hearty meat dishes or rich seafood dishes. Ají, a spicy condiment, is sometimes added, but mouth-burning meals are not the norm.

Pastel de choclo is another dish using corn. Pieces of chicken are covered with a seasoned ground beef mixture to which raisins, black olives and hardboiled eggs are added. This concoction is then topped with a ground corn paste and baked in the oven. Most Chileans then sprinkle it with sugar before eating. Many hearty stews are served as main courses. *Cazuela* has just about everything in it—meat, chicken and/or seafood served in large chunks with a variety of vegetables and rice. Chileans will transfer the ear of corn, meat and potatoes to a plate to eat with a knife and fork, and then eat the broth separately. *Curanto* is another stew typical from the island of Chiloé. It can be made with almost anything—fish, shellfish, meat and/or vegetables. Traditionally the *curanto* is cooked underground in a pit, although today it can sometimes be cooked in pots on a stove.

Empanadas

There are literally hundreds of types of *empanadas* in South America. As the name implies, *empanadas* can be anything covered with a bread-like outer shell. Basically there are two categories of *empanadas*—baked and fried. What is inside is a regional speciality. A typical Chilean *empanada* is filled with a mixture of chopped beef, onion, black olives (sometimes with the pit still inside!), raisins and hardboiled eggs and is called *empanada de pino*. The *pequén empanada* is filled with onions and was originally only eaten by the poor, who could not afford meat. Today it is eaten solely for its flavour. You should also try seafood *empanadas*. Cheese *empanadas* are fried and have a flaky texture. Despite their large size, *empanadas* are usually eaten as an appetiser.

Salads

For those *gringos* who expect iceberg lettuce with a variety of dressings every time the word salad is mentioned, Chile is a shock. Laura finds it consoling to remember that the word *ensalada* (and salad in English) has its roots in Latin, meaning in salt. That is a pretty broad description, and such are salads in Chile. A typical salad is cold vegetables dressed in lemon, vegetable oil and salt. The most common salads are *ensalada chilena* (chopped, peeled tomatoes with sliced onions and cilantro), *ensalada de porotos* (bean salad) and an avocado and celery salad. *Palmitos* (hearts of palm) are also incorporated into a number of salads. *Ensalada rusa* is a mixture of cold boiled potatoes and mayonnaise.

Breads

In many areas of Chile, the tradition of eating bread, bought fresh every morning from the local *panadería*, is still honoured. Some bread sellers even deliver bread to their regular customers' homes every day, although this is becoming less common. Supermarkets normally feature a bakery. Bread is sold by the kilogramme and is never refrigerated. Chileans would consider that an insult. *Chapalele* is a typical bread from Chiloé made from potatoes and wheat flour and boiled. *Milcao* is also made from potatoes and originated in Chiloé. *Sopaipilla* is an unbaked bread made from *zapallo* or Chilean pumpkin. When they are served with a warm caramel sauce they are called *sopaipillas pasadas*. This is usually only eaten in winter when it is cold and rainy because they are supposed to warm you up!

Hallullas, *marraquetas* and *pan amasado* are the most popular varieties of bread found in Chile. *Hallullas* are round, flat pieces of white bread. The *marraqueta* is a small, dense, French type of white bread. Actually, most bread in Chile is somewhat dense. *Pan amasado*, a very traditional bread, is cooked without yeast and therefore is very flat and

If you are looking for something to top your bread try *quesillo*, a light cheese with the consistency of tofu. It is very popular and is served frequently at breakfast and *once*. If you prefer something sweet, *dulce de membrillo*, is sweet quince and has the consistency of hardened jam.

very dense. At the supermarket you will find bins filled with different types of bread. Place your selection in a plastic bag and take it to be weighed and priced before heading to the cashier. *Pan de molde*, sold pre-wrapped, is somewhat fluffy, and is the closest thing to American sandwich bread. Chileans love white bread and it may be more difficult to find wheat or other multigrain breads.

Fruits in Chile are generally eaten with a fork and knife, not with the fingers. For example, an apple is peeled and then sliced and eaten with a fork. Actually, most foods are eaten with silverware, including pizza, sandwiches, french fries, chicken, etc. Only a few appetizers and snacks may be eaten with the fingers.

Desserts

Chileans have a sweet tooth that is only satisfied by very sweet desserts. Even tea and juice are made with great amounts of sugar. Desserts at lunchtime generally consist of canned fruit accompanied by ice cream (called *macedonia*). If you prefer fruit without ice cream, just order compote. An interesting dessert is *leche nevada*, where meringues are added to a

sugary egg yolk and milk mixture, and then frozen. Many desserts have a meringue component, including the various types of *suspiros*. Eggs are also the base for flan, a classic in all Spanish speaking countries, as well as for *leche asada* (a type of flan). *Arroz con leche* is similar to rice pudding.

You cannot talk about desserts in Chile without mentioning *manjar blanco*, aka *dulce de leche*. Basically it is cooked sweetened condensed milk. There is a way to make *manjar blanco* at home by cooking a can of sweetened condensed milk, but you should consult a good recipe book or a Chilean friend before attempting it because

While at the supermarket do not pass up the varieties of refrigerated prepared desserts sold in plastic cups. Nestlé is very big in Chile and all of South America, and does a good job of providing tasty, inexpensive desserts. Europeans may be more familiar with these and other prepared foods available in Chile. For many, they are a welcome addition to the refrigerator.

it can be very dangerous if the can explodes. *Manjar* is spread on bread like peanut butter or Nutella, and the large containers available at the supermarkets testify to the fact that it is extremely popular. It turns up in countless cakes and sweets, such as *panqueque celestino*, crepes, *torta mil hojas* and *manjar relleno*—a sweet doughnut-like fried pastry into which warm *manjar* is poured.

Picarones are Chilean doughnuts and they also come in a *pasados* version with caramel sauce. *Calzones rotos* (yes, torn underwear! in Spanish) are strips of dough with a hole sliced in the middle and one end is pulled through to give it a twisty shape. Then of course there are Spanish *churros*, long, round, fried pastries sprinkled with sugar and cinnamon. On many street corners you will find hawkers selling *cuchuflí*, small tube-like cookies filled with *manjar*.

Chilean Fruit

You'll find some interesting and tasty fruits in Chile. Some of them are listed below:

- *chirimoya* (custard apple), often served fresh. A favourite is *chirimoya alegre*, the fruit is sliced and served in a bowl of orange juice
- papaya, preserved, not fresh, served with its own syrup
- *lúcuma*, never eaten fresh, often used to flavour cakes and ice cream, reminiscent of praline
- *tuna*, prickly pear
- *chupones*, found in the south, offshoot of a type of cactus plant that is chewed
- *plátano*, banana, often served sliced and drizzled with palm tree syrup

---

BEVERAGES
Alcoholic Beverages

One of the first things that people associate with Chile is its wine. The central region of the country has an ideal climate for producing wine—warm summers, rain-free autumns, moderate winters and a mild spring with no frosts to kill young vines. Critics liken Chilean wines to French wines

Throughout most of the year, Chileans enjoy fresh fruits and vegetables.

rather than Californian wines for flavour. In general, Chilean red wines tend to have a stronger reputation than the whites. Interestingly, a grape that was believed to be lost to disease in France was rediscovered in Chile. For many years Carmenère had been mistakenly classified as Merlot. This lovely wine should definitely be sampled and it is worthwhile to become somewhat versed in Chilean wines.

Pisco is a clear spirit similar to brandy. It is produced in the Elqui Valley where the climate is hot, with 300 days a year of clear skies, low rainfall and very little wind. The grapes grown there have a very high sugar content. *Pisco* is popular for mixing with soft drinks like Coca Cola (called *piscola*), ginger ale or vermouth but it is most common in *Pisco* sours. This classic drink is made with lemon juice, sugar, ice and beaten egg white. The Peruvians made this drink famous, but the Chilean version tastes slightly different.

Toasts

Chileans always make a toast with the first drink. It is usually a few words in honour of the host or to mark a special occasion. Glasses are raised, eye contact is made and everyone says "*Salud*" (which means health) in unison. After the initial toast, there may be additional random "*Saluds*" throughout the evening.

Vaina is a tasty mixture of port wine with egg white and cinnamon. *Aguardiente* (fire water) is very strong, and is also made from distilled grapes. It is often served around Christmas in *cola de mono*, a coffee and milk drink. *Chicha*, borrowed from the Amerindians, is made from fermented grapes. It tastes like apple cider and is popular around 18 September, National Day.

Other Beverages

Non-alcoholic beverages are also popular in Chile. Fruit juices made in blenders are common. They are made with either milk or water and may contain a lot of added sugar. When at the grocery store read labels carefully, it can be very trying to find a juice with no added sugars. Soda is consumed in vast quantities in Chile. Most meals are accompanied by juice or soda (*bebidas*) and if you request just plain water, you might not be believed. For the average Chilean *bebidas* are far superior to a glass of plain water. Soft drinks are freely given to children of all ages, and it is not uncommon to see Coca-cola being drunk from a baby bottle by toddlers. If you are invited to a Chilean's home for dinner or to a child's birthday party, be prepared for your child to be offered a soft drink. If you object to your children drinking cola, many Chileans will offer orange soda (Fanta) or a diet soda as an alternative, believing it is healthier.

Yerba mate is very popular in the Southern Cone—Argentina, Chile, Paraguay and Uruguay. It is a ground herb that is set to steep in a cup or gourd and sipped through a metal straw that strains the herb. After supper some Chileans have *mate*, particularly in the south, as it is supposed to be good for digestion. There are many herbal teas to sample in Chile and they are referred to as *aguitas*. They include herbs found in Chile such as *boldo*, *rosa mosqueta*, *cedrón* and *paico*. Mint and *manzanilla* (chamomile) teas are also popular.

RESTAURANTS

Only a few years ago, the selection of restaurants in Chile was quite limited. Aside from typical Chilean fare, you could find only Italian or Chinese restaurants and in the South,

German restaurants. In recent years, however, as Chileans have more money to spend, restaurants have sprung up all over Santiago. The variety and quality of food offered has improved drastically. Today in Santiago, you can enjoy Mexican, Peruvian, American, Thai, Spanish, Brazilian and many other types of cuisine. In Santiago there are a few vegetarian restaurants (El Vegetariano, El Huerto, Café del Patio and El Naturista) that serve very interesting salads, omelettes, and rice dishes accompanied by freshly pureed fruit juices.

When eating out, expect waiters to come right away to ask for your order. However, prompt follow-up service after the food has been served is rare. Foreigners tend to think of this as bad service, but Chileans, on the other hand, would think this was intruding. You have to ask for the check, as Chileans reserve the right to linger over coffee for hours, and

Lomito'n was the first Chilean restaurant chain and is a good option for a quick meal.

bringing the check immediately after finishing would imply that you should leave.

Tap water is not automatically served in Chilean restaurants. It is more common for patrons to order *agua mineral*, *con* or *sin gas* (mineral water, carbonated or non-carbonated). Spicy *ají*, a condiment, is sometimes found on the table. *Pebre*, a mixture of tomatoes, onions, cilantro, vegetable oil and a little chilli that many eat with bread, makes an appearance on every table. It may come as a shock that you must pay extra for lettuce, tomato, mayonnaise, vegetables, potatoes (which are almost never baked in Chile) or extra rolls, etc., to accompany the meal. Note that you must be careful when ordering coffee, as 'café' will come as Nescafé instant coffee. If you want brewed coffee ask for 'café café'. In Chile the tip is not included in the bill, and 10 per cent is normal.

Many men slip away from the office to have a 'coffee with legs' at one of the several cafes where waitresses dress in skimpy attire.

In addition to the large number of new restaurants, fast food chains abound, both Chilean and the familiar foreign chains. The first Chilean chain was Lomito'n, which serves sandwiches and has pictures on the menu to help you make your decision. A common topping on sandwiches is cold sliced green beans. On the subject of sandwiches: a *Barros Luco* is a grilled steak and cheese sandwich; a *Barros Jarpa* is a grilled ham and cheese sandwich. A *Completo* is a hot-dog with everything, while an *Especial* is a basic hot-dog. Stemming from the German tradition, a popular topping on hot-dogs is *chukrut* (sauerkraut). Chileans do not share tables at restaurants and even at fast food restaurants they would prefer to sit alone.

Café Haití is a chain of coffee houses that has become a Chilean institution. Concentrated in downtown Santiago, patrons, predominantly men, stand at the counter and drink coffee. The trick is that the waitresses are dressed in the tightest and shortest dresses you've ever seen. This has led to a common expression in Chile, '*Café con piernas*' or 'A coffee with legs'. This gimmick spawned a number of imitators and there are now many coffee houses where the women wear sleazy lingerie.

GROCERY STORES

In cities of any considerable size in Chile, supermarkets are well-stocked and often cheaper than the open-air street *ferias*. Imported goods are available at many supermarkets, however, sometimes in limited amounts. Jumbo, a 'hyper-market', has the largest selection of imported items, with many products from the United States and Europe, especially Germany. Lider is another hypermarket that in addition to food sells clothes and household items. Milk is generally whole in Chile, but skim is available. As with juice, milk comes in boxes that need no refrigeration until opened.

At the entrance to the supermarket you will notice a large bottle return section. Most beer and carbonated beverages come in glass or heavy plastic bottles marked *retornable*, for which you will be required to pay a small deposit. You are entitled to the deposit when returning the bottle, but you need to have your original receipt. Most people just get credit towards the purchase of another bottle. You will be given a slip of paper with the number of bottles returned which allows you to purchase the exact number of bottles without paying an additional deposit. Keep the piece of paper as you must give it to the cashier when checking out. In small neighbourhood stores just return the bottles when you buy more, no slip will be issued.

Generally, a young boy or girl will bag your groceries. He or she may not be an employee of the store, so it is correct to give a tip for the service, even if you did not request it. While at the check-out, make sure that you get all your items, as sometimes there is confusion as to which items belong to whom.

If you want local colour not available in a supermarket, head to the Mercado Central. Located in downtown Santiago, it is the place to go for fresh seafood. The building's architecture was inspired by Eiffel. It is very old with small

For fresh and exotic seafood in Santiago, visit the Mercado Central.

booths where stall owners can even cook the food for you to eat right there. For fresh produce, many people in Santiago go to La Vega Central located near the Mapocho River. Groceries, produce and fresh flowers are sold wholesale and retail. On weekends, *ferias* or fruit and vegetable markets are set up in most neighbourhoods. Produce fresh from the countryside is sold and it is well worth the extra stop.

In season, fruit and vegetables are cheap and very flavourful. You must remember to weigh your fruit and vegetables in the supermarkets in the special weighing section, not at the check-out. All vegetables and fruit should be washed in disinfectant solution that can be bought in the supermarkets because of the heavy use of pesticides. Tap water in Chile contains levels of bacteria that could upset the foreigner's stomach, especially upon arrival. Chileans may swear that your water is safe, but they are immune to the problem. Many foreigners, however, do drink tap water without incident. Just remember that juice and ice in Chile are both made with tap water, so only consume them if you feel confident.

ENJOYING THE CULTURE

'I was reading a book, its cover was made of metal, its pages of gold, its letters of coral. Crying, I deciphered legends, yellow, black and red, page by page...'
—Violeta Parra, songwriter/folksinger, *Cuecas del Libro*

CHILEAN CULTURE

On the surface, Chile appears to be not all that different from the United States or parts of Europe. Yet, once you begin to dig around, you'll find a rich culture that makes Chile unique. Even though the society is relatively homogeneous, several extremely different traditions come together to shape Chilean culture. Chileans are very proud of their customs, many of which go back hundreds of years. If you make an effort to learn about this special history and are a willing participant, you will be aptly rewarded.

The Mapuche

Before the Spaniards arrived, the Mapuche ruled a large portion of the territory now known as Chile, in essence the entire central section. Although not the only indigenous group in the country, the Mapuche are perhaps the first or only native people to come to mind when thinking of Chile. Originally, the Mapuche—called Araucanos by the *conquistadors*—lived on Chiloé Island and the surrounding mainland to the north and south in both Chile and Argentina. The term *Mapuche* (people of the land) encompasses most of the peoples native to central Chile including the *Williche* (people of the south), *Pikunche* (people of the north), *Puelche* (people of the East), the *Lafkenche* (people of the coast) and *Pehuenche* (people of the Pehuen).

Ethnically and linguistically the Mapuche were one people, but the vast length of their territory gave rise to differences in dialect and customs. Those on Chiloé were sedentary and monogamous fishermen and farmers, while those on the mainland were polygamous nomadic fishermen, farmers and herdsmen. The Mapuche believed that while they could own personal property, the land and the animals were for the common benefit of the clan. Early chronicles describe open lands with rolling hills. The forests were kept in check by the grazing livestock. However, after smallpox and war decimated the Mapuche, forests reclaimed the land.

The family head was called *Cacique* or *Lonko*, and could have as many as 10 wives as a sign of his power. The Mapuche lived in family groups of up to 500 members. The *Caciques* formed alliances with other family groups for trade, but there was no central government. This, and the fact that they did not have permanent villages, saved the Mapuche from early subordination by the Spanish. While the society was ultimately led by men, medicine women, called *Machi*, were very powerful and as important to society as the Mapuche chiefs. Until today, women in general are held in high esteem and play a major role in their religion. According to Mapuche tradition, only women can communicate directly with the gods.

The spirituality of native Amerindians in general is profound, and the Mapuches are no exception. Although they have no temples, Mapuches believe that there are positive and negative forces present in every act. They look for divine intervention in all aspects of their lives. The significant forces of life, love and creation are represented by Ngenechen, while death and destruction are embodied in Wekufu. Although the Mapuche accept that divine spirits are everywhere, they nevertheless believe in the existence of a supreme being called *Guinechen* (master of the land). The east represents the positive forces and therefore plays an important role in the lives of the Mapuche. In fact, Mapuche dwellings, called *rukas*, always face east.

One of the most well-known Mapuche festivals is Ngillatun. It is a prayer ceremony to invoke the spirit Pillán to ensure

a good harvest. The Machi leads the ceremony and uses a *rewe* (ladder to heaven) that also faces east. The whole town participates with singing and dancing and in the past an animal was sacrificed. Participants paint their faces blue and white, sacred colours which hold positive meanings. Afterwards there is a big party and the Mapuches celebrate by eating and drinking lots of *chicha*.

Several unique instruments can be found in Mapuche culture. The *trutruka* is a very long type of trumpet that makes a loud monotone sound. The Machi play the *cultrún*, a type of drum decorated with cosmic designs, during rituals. For sport the Mapuche play a game called *chueca*, which is similar to field hockey, using a wooden ball.

Every culture has its own explanation for the creation of the world. According to Mapuche legend, their land was formed when two snakes met while crawling across a flat land. Kai Kai was a terrific snake that scared other animals. Treng Treng had the respect of the animals, but they were not afraid of him. Eventually they met in battle. Kai Kai won, but his hissing created an ocean that threatened all life. To save himself and the other animals, Treng Treng piled mounds of earth into mountains. The animals that were not strong enough to climb up fell into the sea to become fish. The animals that climbed the highest and the fastest became humans. After the flood, the humans settled in the fertile valley between Treng Treng's mountains and Kai Kai's ocean, and they called themselves Mapuche. They believe that the frequent tremors in Chile are due to the thrashing snakes.

Of course, the Mapuches of modern Chile have evolved into a culture somewhat distinct from that of centuries ago. Even on the reservations the Chilean national culture has a firm foothold, mostly brought in by the extension of primary education. A survey of Mapuche on four southern reservations found that less than 10 per cent were monolingual Mapuche, around 50 per cent spoke both Spanish and Mapuche in their homes, and 40 per cent spoke only Spanish. Almost all Mapuche under 30 are literate in Spanish.

This sculpture in Santiago's main square honors Chile's indigenous ancestry.

Mapuche traditionally wear brightly coloured handwoven clothes, which the women accessorise with the fine silver jewellery for which they are known. However, today they generally wear western clothes when not on the reservations.

Mapuche are well known for their silver work and you can buy such items in Santiago and Temuco. They started using silver after the arrival of the Spanish, who brought the precious metal with them. The intricate pieces are related to their religious beliefs and are generally worn during rituals. Certain pieces are used as a safeguard against evil and others as a symbol of fertility. Mapuche silversmiths make earrings, necklaces, pendants, *ponchón* (similar to a stick pin) and items to decorate the hair. The distinctive pieces are large and flat with tubes, chains and links.

Tribes of the Extreme South

A number of different tribes once lived at the southernmost part of the continent. The Chonos inhabited the area known today as Aisén. The Kawèsqar (Alacaluf) were a nomadic tribe that moved along the channels in the far south in their canoes. The Aonikenk lived and roamed along the steppes of the southern Andes. The Selk'nam (Ona) lived in the northern parts of Tierra del Fuego and the Yagan (Yamana) lived along the southern coast near the Beagle Channel. Due to the severe cold, many of the indigenous peoples in southern Chile wore large pelts wrapped around their feet. The Spanish explorers referred to them as *Patagones* (big feet) and that is how the region became known as Patagonia. When Magellan sailed through the strait that now bears his name, he and his crew saw a great many bonfires used by the natives for warmth and cooking. They called the area Tierra del Fuego (land of fire), which is how such a cold region earned its hot name. Today, most of these groups are considered culturally extinct. Living in such an isolated part of the country, their customs and beliefs did not make a huge impact on Chilean society. Now that the groups have all but disappeared, their culture is, for the most part, relegated to museums and history books.

NATIVE PEOPLES OF THE NORTH

In addition to the Aymara, the Atacameños, Quechua and Kollas are indigenous tribes that live in the northern part of Chile. Their numbers dwindled following the Spanish conquest and the formation of the Chilean state, a consequence of extermination, disease and inclusion into mainstream society. The Diaguitas also lived in the north and their pottery stands out as the best of all the indigenous groups of Chile.

Aymara

The Aymara inhabit the extreme northern part of Chile and are part of the larger group of Aymara that also live in Bolivia and parts of Peru. The Aymara reside primarily in the altiplano (mountain plateau) and live off the land, growing crops and raising livestock, including llamas. Many travel frequently to the cities, while some have moved there permanently. They have maintained their language, although they also speak Spanish. Considered full members of Chilean society, they continue to celebrate their own special rituals. Some ceremonies are purely indigenous while many others are a mixture of indigenous and Catholic beliefs. Pachamama, Mother Earth, is often honoured in their rituals. One of the better-known traditions is carnival, a blend of Aymara and Catholic traditions. It is a celebration of excess prior to the abstinence of Lent and has been heavily influenced by carnivals in Bolivia and Peru. The festival is observed by Indians and non-Indians alike, but only in the north. Carnival is not celebrated in central or southern Chile.

La Tirana

The festival of La Tirana has its origins with the Amerindians in the north, but today all are invited to participate. The festival takes place over three days each July in La Tirana, a village 70 km (43 miles) from the city of Iquique. During the festival the population swells from 5,000 to over 70,000. La Tirana has been strongly influenced by the Bolivian Carnival celebrations, particularly the one in Oruro.

The village is named after an Incan princess who was converted to Catholicism by her Spanish lover. She was the daughter of the high priest of the Sun Temple in Cuzco, although she lived in what is now Chile. After watching her father murdered by *conquistadors*, she killed any Spaniard who came near her or her people and gained the nickname of *La Tirana del Tamarugal* (the Tyrant of the land of Tamarugo trees).

One night a silver miner named Vasco de Almeida was captured. It had been the rule to kill all Spaniards, but the princess fell in love with him, and through him learned the Christian concept of eternal life after death. She converted to Christianity in order to be united forever with de Almeida in the next life. The princess was baptised with the name María. Soon after, she imposed Catholicism on her people by force. María and her husband were eventually killed by angry mobs. As she lay dying, she begged to be buried with her husband at the place where she had been baptised. The grave was marked with a cross.

Years later a priest found the cross, and upon hearing the legend built a temple in honour of the *Virgen del Carmen of La Tirana*. This sanctuary is the end point of the colourful procession of *chinos*, the highlight of the festival. *Chinos* are brotherhoods that call themselves guardians of the Virgin Mary. (In spite of their name, which means the Chinese, their practices have nothing to do with Chinese culture.) These societies wear special uniforms that resemble those of *conquistadors*, Indians, ancient Romans or other groups. They dance and chant divinities similar to prayers from Spain during the ceremony.

Easter Island and the Rapa Nui

Easter Island or Isla de Pascua is shrouded in mystery. A group of Polynesians, the Rapa Nui, first settled on the island around AD 400, led there in bark canoes by Hotu Matua, the king. As the population grew, a clan society developed based upon the extended family. The family unit jointly owned and cultivated the land and each clan was led by a chief (*ariki*). Crop production required relatively little time and labour,

which allowed the islanders to devote much time and energy to ceremonial activities. Priests, scribes and artists were important to cultural development.

Easter Island is most famous for its Moais, large stones carved in the shape of predominantly male heads and torsos. The Moais are thought to represent dead chiefs or gods. There are also over 300 large stone platforms thought to be altars, called *ahu*. They were used for burials, ancestor worship and to commemorate past chiefs. Some are astronomically aligned, indicating an advanced degree of knowledge.

Rongorongo is a hieroglyphic script that was found inscribed on many wooden tablets and staffs in 1864. It is the only indigenous Oceania script found to have existed before the 20th century. The glyphs themselves are very small, about 1 centimetre in height, and portray humans, birds, fish and plants. Every other line is written upside down so that the tablet must be inverted to continue reading. By 1866, only two years later, most of the tablets had been burnt, hidden or used for boat planks or fishing implements. Today, only about 20 tablets remain and no one has been able to successfully decipher them.

The island was also home to thousands of petroglyphs. Most of these rock carvings depict birds, animals and birdmen. The birdman (Tangata Manu) figures prominently in Easter Island folklore. This creature has a bird's head and a man's body and holds an egg in one hand. The cult of the birdman originated near Orongo. He was said to be an earthly representative of the creator god called Makemake. Each spring, a contest was held between the clans. A representative swam from Orongo to Motu Nui, a small islet nearby. The goal was to find the first egg laid by the Manu Tara, a sacred bird. During the search, other members of the tribe made offerings and prayed to Makemake. The winner was the first person to swim back to Orongo and present his chief with the egg. This chief was then named 'birdman' for the year and led a procession to Rano Raraku where he lived in seclusion and enjoyed the favour of Makemake.

The Pascuenses (the Spanish term for the islanders) are also known for their wood carvings, the most famous being the Moai Kavakava (image of ribs). The small statue depicts a bearded man with his ribs sticking out. It is believed to represent the spirits of dead ancestors, called Aku Aku. According to legend, Chief Tuu-ko-ihu saw two of these spirits one night and they later appeared to him in a dream. The people of Easter Island tattooed almost every part of their bodies. Faces, necks, chests, abdomens, backs, and legs were adorned with geometrical designs, and human or bird forms.

The Rapa Nui relate the story of their arrival on the island through the use of a game using string figures. These are called *kai kai*. The player forms a figure using a piece of string and through different finger movements is able to alter the figure. Meanwhile, the player sings a song describing how the original settlers built boats, sailed across the ocean to Rapa Nui and then dismantled the boats to build their first homes.

When the first Europeans arrived they did not find a flourishing civilisation. Instead, they found a culture in decline. It is believed that as the society grew and developed, the island's population reached 7,000. However, this growth

placed a heavy burden on the island's ecosystem. The island had been almost completely forested when the first settlers arrived. Land was continuously cleared for agricultural purposes, for fuel and to build houses and canoes. Most importantly, however, large tree trunks had been used to move the giant Moais across the island after they had been carved. Deforestation caused soil erosion and crops were insufficient to feed the large population. The islanders were forced to live in caves and the lack of wood meant that no canoes could be built. They were trapped on an island that could no longer provide for them. The clans turned upon each other and it is believed that the Moais were knocked down during these wars.

The Europeans found an island without trees. The population had already dwindled but the Peruvian slave raids in the 1860s and diseases introduced by the Europeans such as smallpox reduced the number of people by 90 per cent. By 1877, only 111 people remained. The king, his son and the priests had all been captured as slaves. Without them, the Europeans were unable to learn about the island's culture and history. This led to the invention of many stories of extraterrestrial activity and submerged cities to explain the existence of the Moais. Although these theories have been ruled out, this vibrant culture will always remain somewhat of a mystery.

In late January or early February, the people of Easter Island celebrate Tapati. This festival honours the Rapa Nui culture with native dance, chants and song and various competitions in woodcarving, spear fishing, horse racing and Kai Kai.

Chiloé

The island of Chiloé is the richest part of Chile in terms of mythology and legends. Many are derived from Indian beliefs mixed with the Spanish-Christian tradition. Christian beliefs come into play with good fighting evil. The isolation and inclement weather of the island work to create this mysticism. Ask a Chilean about Chiloé and they will tell you about *brujos* (wizards), who belong to a secret society. To be accepted as a member of a society, a candidate must kill a close relative and perform other evil acts, from which they acquire immense magical powers. *Brujos* can fly, but only when wearing a vest made out of the skin of a virgin turned inside out. If you are in Chiloé and accidentally put on your sweater inside out, Chileans will ask you if you are planning to fly.

Most mythological beings are associated with *brujos*: Invunche, the guardian of the *brujos'* lair, is a baby whose limbs have all been broken and whose orifices have been sealed. Caleuche, a mythological ship, is the vessel of the *brujos* that appears at night and aboard which they enjoy a never-ending party. Pincoya and Pincoy, Chiloé's sirens, are half fish, half human. Trauco, a gnome with no feet, is blamed for impregnating young, unwed women. A friend was staying with a family in Chiloé and the parents seriously spoke of the trauco who had

A popular event in Chiloé is a *minga*, which brings the entire community together to help a neighbour. There are mingas for planting, harvesting, fixing the church, etc. One of the most common *mingas* is to move an entire house. The house is mounted on tree trunks and pulled by oxen to the new site. The house can even be moved across the sea! When the house has arrived at its new location, the owner treats everyone to lots of food and drink in appreciation.

gotten their young daughter pregnant. There are dozens of other legends and creatures and ample books written on the subject.

Public Holidays in Chile

1 January	New Year's Day
March/April	Good Friday
1 May	Labour Day
21 May	Navy Day, Iquique Naval Battle
May/June	Corpus Christi
29 June	Feast Day of St. Peter and St. Paul
15 August	Assumption
18 September	Independence Day
19 September	Army Day
12 October	Columbus Day
1 November	All Saint's Day
8 December	Immaculate Conception
25 December	Christmas

Certain holidays that fall on a weekend will be celebrated on the following Monday.

FIESTAS PATRIAS

National Day

Fiestas Patrias is a two-day holiday (18 September is National Day and 19 September is Army Day) that celebrates people's sense of 'Chilean-ness'. Everyone is in a festive mood and bursting with national pride. Chilean flags are flown throughout the country (the only month when this is allowed) and its colours of red, blue and white seem to grace everything. It is a great time to be in Chile and allows you an opportunity to see into the soul of the country. On 18 September, more commonly referred to as *el dieciocho*, many Chileans celebrate the day with an *asado* (barbeque) at home or at the home of friends or family.

September is springtime in Chile, a perfect time for a fiesta. People are ready to celebrate after a chilly, wet winter. During this month, kites suddenly appear and are sold on every street corner. Kite-flying competitions are held and some of the *comisiones* or battles can be fierce. The strings are coated with pulverised glass and the objective is to cut loose your opponent's kite.

At an *asado*, Chileans feast on lots of red meat, accompanied by an assortment of fresh salads. Later that night, many may choose to visit the *fondas*.

Fondas are fairs set up all over the country in the weeks preceding 18 September. Many tents serve food including *empanadas* (meat or cheese filled turnovers), *anticuchos* (shish kebabs), *carne asada* (grilled beef and pork) and drinks, such as *chicha* (fermented grape punch) and *pisco* (grape brandy). Larger tents at the *fonda* feature live music and dancing. Folk music makes a strong appearance and everyone seems to be dancing the *cueca*.

Cueca

Cueca is the national dance of Chile. You can recognise a *cueca* by the handkerchiefs that are elaborately waved above the couple's heads. The characteristics of the dance depend on the region, but generally the couple face each other and dance back and forth and around each other while waving the handkerchief. *Cueca* is usually accompanied by a guitar, and sometimes a harp, accordion, piano and tambourine. In the north, a brass or reed band is sometimes the accompaniment. The spectators keep time by clapping.

Most Chileans will tell you that *cueca* evokes the mating ritual of hens and roosters and there is a good basis for this observation. The *cueca* is a courtship dance, but for all the sensual interpretation, it does not seem to be a very sexy dance. *Cueca* is no *lambada* with erotic pelvic thrusts! The couple do not touch while dancing *cueca*. If you go to a *fonda*, no doubt you will be invited to dance the *cueca*. Don't be shy! It's a fun and easy way of showing Chileans how much you enjoy their country.

Army Day
Army Day is celebrated with a large military parade at Parque O'Higgins, in Santiago. The parade is televised live on all channels and lasts about four hours. Every division of the Armed Forces and Carabineros is represented. There is an unofficial competition among the baton leaders of each of the four military academies to see who can goose-step the highest. Other highlights include the army mountain troops,

dressed in white uniforms complete with skis strapped across their back and Saint Bernard dogs. The commandos can be recognised by their *corvos*, knives especially designed to disembowel an adversary. Some parade in period uniform. These troops invaded southern Peru during the War of the Pacific and became notorious for the use of these knives. Even today mothers in southern Peru warn their children not of the boogieman, but of the terrible Chilean.

HUASO CULTURE

During Fiestas Patrias you will see a greater than normal number of people dressed as *Huasos*. The Chilean cowboy, or

Chilean children dress up like Huasos during Fiestas Patrias.

huaso, is not relegated to history because his culture is alive and flourishing. The term *huaso* is believed to come from an Indian word for shoulders or haunches. As the Mapuche had never seen horses before the Spanish conquest, they assumed that the rider was attached to the horse between the shoulder and the haunch. Of course the Mapuche soon discovered the truth, and went on to become formidable horsemen themselves. *Huasos* live and work in the Central Valley where cattle are raised. The *huaso* zone begins in Santiago and extends southward.

Huaso Outfits

The elegant *huaso* outfit is a Chilean version of the Andalusian traditional dress for men. On his head he wears a broad and flat rimmed hat, called a *chupalla*, made of straw in the summer, and felt in the winter. A basic white shirt and black or gray pin-striped trousers are the foundation for his outfit. Over the shirt a short brown or black jacket is worn. The rider's calves are sheathed in black leather leggings decorated with long leather tassels. These chaps are called *perneras* (derived from the Spanish word for leg, pierna) and fit over the riding boots and pants. Perneras are used to protect the *huaso's* legs when riding through thick brush. He wears high black boots with a heel to accommodate large spurs. These spurs, sometimes made of silver, have rowels or spiked discs used to prod the flanks of the horse to make it go faster. Traditionally, *huasos* complete their attire with a *manta*, a colourful short poncho they wear over their clothing.

Rodeos

Huasos usually work alone or with a few others when tending the cattle. Their solitude is broken up by rodeo competitions (there are over 200 rodeo clubs in Chile). At first, these rodeos were an annual event when workers rounded up the cattle to count and brand the animals for sale. Eventually they evolved into festivals where animals were brought to the village main square and riders displayed their talents. Today they are a contest of skill in cattle herding. Taking their place in the celebration of all things Chilean, rodeos are very popular during Fiestas Patrias. The rodeo season starts in September and runs through May.

For the last 150 years or so rodeo has been a sport with definite rules. Unlike rodeos in other countries, there is no roping or riding of untamed bulls and calves. The *huaso* is part of a team, including a horse and a partner. The horses were brought by the Spanish and are unique to Chile—not too tall, yet strong and intelligent. Before the actual rodeo begins the riders perform individual tests of agility. These tests are judged and scored. There is a series of exercises; first the *huaso* walks his mount on a loose rein to prove the gait of the horse, which should be constant, firm and rapid. Then the horse and rider gallop back and forth in a straight line making dramatic about-faces, which the horse should make by turning its body while on its hind legs. Figure eights and circles test the speed and handling of the horses. Just when the mount has become excited, it must calm down as the rider dismounts and walks several paces away. The horse must remain perfectly motionless or it loses points.

The *huaso* rodeo consists of only one event—calf-pinning. *Huasos* have elevated this competition to a complex art form. The *huaso* rodeo takes place in a 40-metre arena. The ring is divided into two parts, each called a *medialuna* or half-moon. A pair of *huasos* enters the *medialuna* and wait for the young bull. This calf, like the bulls at the corridas in Spain, is supposed to have never entered a *medialuna* before to safeguard the purity of its reactions. Although the *huaso* team works together, they do not have equal responsibilities while attempting to pin the calf. One horseman must guide the calf around the *medialuna* while the other follows behind the calf pushing. The pair must herd the calf around the ring twice before pinning it against a specially marked area of the railing. Each rider has three turns to pin the calf against the timber fence. Then the riders change places and run in the opposite direction, repeating the performance in reverse. All this happens while the audience cheers, listens to live folk music, eats *empanadas*, drinks wine and chooses the 'Queen' of the Rodeo.

Cuasimodo

Huasos also play an integral role in the religious festival of Cuasimodo. Observed on the Sunday following Easter Sunday, Cuasimodo is celebrated throughout the entire central region of Chile. The name comes from the Latin words that signal the beginning of mass on this day. The local Catholic priest, riding in a carriage, leads a procession through the community, administering Communion to the homebound. The priest is accompanied by hundreds of *huasos* riding horses and carrying religious images. The *huasos* wear traditional dress but remove their hats and tie kerchiefs around their heads as a sign of respect. The festival originated in the 1800s when *huasos* accompanied priests travelling through sparsely populated areas in order to protect them from thieves. Today, many children participate in the process along with the *huasos*. Instead of riding horses, they ride bicycles that have been elaborately decorated with brightly coloured paper and streamers.

Tijerales

The *tijerales* custom is widespread throughout Chile. *Tijerales* is the Spanish word for the roof support structure of a building. On all construction sites, regardless of whether it is a small house in a rural area or a major skyscraper, when the *tijerales* has been completed a flag is placed on the roof. There is a pause in construction and a barbeque is held for all those involved. Completing the *tijerales* symbolises that the final stage of construction has finally been reached.

NAVY DAY

Although Navy Day (May 21) is not celebrated with the same fanfare as Fiestas Patrias, it stirs up similar feelings of national pride. This day honours the heroism and courage of Arturo Prat, the Chilean Navy's main hero. The anniversary of the Naval Battle of Iquique falls on 21 May. The battle took place in 1879 during the War of the Pacific. Captain Prat, outnumbered and certain to be defeated by Peruvian ships, refused to surrender. He and his crew members died fighting after boarding an enemy vessel. News of this act of bravery served as a catalyst for the Chilean people and was a turning point in the war, which Chile eventually won. The president makes an annual 'State of the Nation' address on this day as Congress opens for a new session. The Mensaje Presidencial recounts the achievements of the past year and lays out the administration's future plans for the country. The speech is aired live on television and radio.

CATHOLIC FESTIVALS

Chilean society's religious character also played a significant part in the formation of the country's traditions and culture. Chile is a predominantly Catholic country and as such, celebrates a number of religious holidays.

Semana Santa

Many Chileans attend church during Holy Week, which culminates with Easter Sunday. Good Friday is an official holiday and offices are closed. The week leading up to Easter Sunday is a somber time for Christians and this is reflected in the mood of the people. During Holy Week children pull dolls representing Judas around the neighbourhood in little carts. They visit houses asking for coins to symbolise the money Judas received for betraying Jesus. At the end of the day, the doll is burned.

Easter Sunday, however, is the holiest day for Catholics and is a cause for rejoicing and celebration. Many Chileans spend the day in their homes with their families after attending religious services. Chileans of German decent traditionally mark the day with Easter egg hunts. Recently this custom has spread to the rest of society.

Festival de San Pedro

On 29 June, or the first Sunday following it, the tiny fishing village of Horcón, about 150 km (93 miles) north of Santiago, celebrates the festival of San Pedro (Saint Peter). All the fishing boats, as well as the village, are gaily decorated. Musical groups called *chinos* from Horcón and other nearby villages dance in devotion to St Peter, while an image of the patron saint of fishermen is carried around the bay. It is believed that Saint Peter will bless them with bountiful fish harvests. Similar festivities are held in Valparaíso and in many other coves along the Chilean coast.

All Saints' Day

On 1 November, many Chileans visit the cemetery to pay their respects to the dead. When this holiday falls near the weekend, it also signals the unofficial beginning of summer and Santiaguinos flock to the beach.

HALLOWEEN

Halloween has not been a traditional event in Chile. However, as the world gets smaller and ideas are introduced from other countries, customs change and develop. You will now see Halloween costumes for sale in parts of Santiago. Although trick-or-treating (the practice of going house to house to ask for candy) has no history in Chile, it has begun to catch on in the wealthier parts of Santiago.

Immaculate Conception

Catholics celebrate the Immaculate Conception on 8 December. A number of Chileans make pilgrimages on this day. One of the biggest pilgrimages entails walking from Santiago to the Santuario de la Virgen de lo Vásquez 86 km (53 miles) away to pray to the Virgin Mary. Lo Vásquez is a shrine to the Blessed Virgin on the main highway between Santiago and the twin cities of Viña del Mar and Valparaíso. Many people stop to visit the shrine throughout the year because it is believed that all prayers to the Virgen de lo Vásquez will be answered. There is a wall in the courtyard covered with plaques thanking and praising the Virgin Mary for answering their petitions. Most children receive their First Communion on this day.

Christmas

In Chile, Christmas is a much more relaxed holiday than in other parts of the world. There is a Christmas spirit, but one is not overwhelmed with Christmas decorations, except in the shopping malls. Santa Claus makes his appearance, dying in the summer heat in his heavy, red suit. Chileans adorn their homes with nativity scenes and Christmas trees, both real and artificial, a tradition brought to Chile by the Germans.

Christmas, like most holidays, is family oriented with an emphasis on children. Families attend midnight mass, and open presents on Christmas Eve. On Christmas Day families gather for an *asado* or spend the day at the beach. It is traditional to serve *pan de pascua* (Christmas Bread), which, unlike fruit cake in the US, is devoured immediately, and *cola de mono*, a Christmas liqueur.

New Year's Eve

At the end of December, the city of Valparaíso celebrates the Cultural Carnival. Known as the Cultural Capital of Chile, the city fills up with artists, performers and tourists. For about a week you can enjoy music, dance, film and theatre. The events culminate with a spectacular fireworks display on New Year's Eve. At midnight, fireworks light up the skies throughout the country, but the show that explodes over the Pacific Ocean in Valparaíso is the most spectacular.

New Year's Eve is a very festive occasion. It takes place in the middle of the summer and is celebrated with *asados* (barbeques) and family gatherings. Some people spend this holiday at the beach. At the stroke of midnight, while the fireworks are exploding overhead, Chileans embrace to wish each other Happy New Year, *Feliz Año Nuevo* or simply *Feliz Año*. Never wish a Chilean Happy New Year in advance because it is considered unlucky. Many people will eat a spoonful of lentils for good luck. Others put money and bus or plane tickets in their pockets to ensure wealth and travel in the coming year. After celebrating the stroke of midnight with family, many people set out to visit friends until the wee hours of the morning.

MUSIC FESTIVALS

Summers seem to be filled with holidays and festivals. The Festival de la Canción de Viña del Mar is one of the most important popular music festivals in the Spanish-speaking world. It takes place every year in the seaside resort town of Viña del Mar, not far from Santiago. It is primarily a contest for up-and-coming singers, yet is well known for the big name international artists who headline the festival. The audience is loud and enthusiastic. It is broadcast on television throughout Latin America. Although the festival has been criticised for not including enough Chilean bands and for emphasising mainstream Spanish pop music, it is nevertheless the main event of the summer in Viña, and for that matter in Chile. The Song Festival is held in the beginning of February. It lasts for one week, with two performances daily, one in the afternoon and the other at night. More than 30,000 spectators fill the Quinta Vergara outdoor auditorium. The winner is presented with the Gaviota (seagull) Trophy. The audience decides what performers get the Antorcha (torch) Trophy for their stage appeal.

The Semanas Musicales de Frutillar is another large musical event. It is a 10-day classical music festival held in

Traditional Andean instruments like the *zampoña* (pan flute) have been incorporated into current Chilean popular music.

the town of Frutillar near Puerto Montt in southern Chile. It begins the first week of February and highlights both Chilean and foreign classical musicians alike.

The Pop Music Festival de La Serena (January), the Folk Music Festival de la Patagonia, in Punta Arenas (July) and the Folk Festival del Huaso in Olmué, Central Chile (January) are also well-known musical events.

Claudio Arrau

Claudio Arrau was an internationally acclaimed classical pianist who was born in the city of Chillán in 1903. He later moved to Europe to study and remained there until his death in 1991 in Austria. His recordings of numerous compositions by the masters, including all of Beethoven's *Sonatas* are highly praised and respected.

CONTEMPORARY MUSIC

The Chilean music scene has something for every taste, from traditional Chilean music and folksongs to blues, jazz and rock. Chile is probably best known for its popular folk groups. Inti Illimani is the most internationally celebrated Chilean band. Los Inti, as they are affectionately referred to in Chile, went into exile to Europe like many other artists during the military regime. Originally a protest folk group which used traditional Andean instruments, over time Inti Illimani's music and arrangements have become much more sophisticated. They have incorporated elements of Latin American and European folk music with New Age and even classical music. No drive through the Andes is complete without Inti Illimani playing in the background. For those who don't understand much Spanish, listen to their instrumental CD *Imagination*.

Quilapayún is the quintessential protest song folk group. It was very combative early on and some of its songs were anthems for the revolution, for instance *La Batea*. Quilapayún also went into exile in Europe, where its members remain. With the passage of time their songs have softened somewhat from their original hard-line stance. Illapu is another group that incorporates Andean sounds into popular music. Originally, their songs too, were politically charged. On the other side of the political spectrum, Los Huasos Quincheros represented the conservative right and sang folk songs for the upper classes. They are the very definition of *cuico*.

New Song Movement

Perhaps the most famous Chilean singer/songwriter was Violeta Parra. She was the mother of the New Song Movement, a cultural movement that swept the country in the late 1960s and early 1970s. It voiced the great hopes for political and social change in Latin America by incorporating traditional rhythms, instruments and musical forms with modern lyrics. The New Song Movement inspired and influenced many later musicians. Parra committed suicide in 1967, supposedly due to financial problems and the failure of a love affair. Her most famous song *Gracias a la Vida* (Thanks to Life) was also recorded and made popular in English by Joan Baez. Her brother Nicanor Parra is a famous poet and several other family members are well-known musicians.

Another prominent member of the New Song Movement was the folk singer Víctor Jara. He was arrested during the coup and detained in the Estadio Chile. He bravely sang protest songs while being detained and was eventually killed. He is a martyr to many Chileans. The Chile Stadium was renamed Estadio Víctor Jara in his honour. His two most famous songs are the beautiful *Te recuerdo Amanda* and *Plegaria del Labrador*.

Popular Music

Chilean youth enjoy listening to both English and Spanish language pop and rock music. There is no shortage of radio stations and television programmes dedicated to playing the latest hits. While Chile has had some very successful rock groups like Lucybell, Los Prisioneros, Los Jaivas, La Ley and Los Tres (the latter two now disbanded) it is not a serious contender in the Latin American pop scene.

FINE ART

Chile has produced several world-renowned artists, whose works have been exhibited in Latin America, Europe and

North America. Perhaps the most famous, is the surrealist painter Roberto Matta. Other prominent artists include Nemesio Antúnez, Arturo Duclós, Samy Benmayor, Bororo, Alfredo Jaar, José Balmes, Gracia Barrios and Gonzalo Cienfuegos. Fine examples of Chilean and international art are on display at the Museo de Bellas Artes (Fine Arts Musem) and the Museo de Arte Contemporáneo (Contemporary Art Museum) in Santiago.

Museums in Chile

- Museo Nacional de Bellas Artes (Fine Arts Museum) Parque Forestal, Santiago
- Museo de Arte Contemporáneo (Contemporary Art Museum) Parque Forestal, Santiago
- Museo Chileno de Arte Pre-Colombino (Museum of Pre-Colombian Art) Bandera 361, Santiago
- Casa Colorado y Museo de Santiago (Red House and Santiago Museum) Merced 860, Santiago
- Museo de Arte Colonial San Francisco (San Francisco Church and Museum of Colonial Art) Londres 4, Santiago
- Quinta Normal Park. Houses Museo Ferroviario (Railway Museum), Museo de Ciencia y Tecnología (Museum of Science and Technology), Artequin Museum and Museo Nacional de Historia Natural (Museum of Natural History).
- Museo Interactivo Mirador (MIM) Avenida Sebastopol 90, Parque Brasil, Santiago. Hands-on children's museum.
- Museo de Arte Popular Americano (Museum of American Folk Art) Compañía 2691, Santiago
- La Chascona (Pablo Neruda's House) Fernando Márquez de la Plata 0192, Bellavista, Santiago
- Isla Negra (Pablo Neruda's home on the coast)
- Museo de Bellas Artes de Viña del Mar (Museum of Fine Arts of Viña del Mar) Palacio Vergara, Viña del Mar.
- Museo Antropológico P. Sebastián Englert (Rapa Nui Museum), Tahai, Easter Island
- Museo Arqueológico Padre Le Paige, San Pedro de Atacama.

LITERATURE

Poets

Chileans have made huge contributions to Spanish literature. In fact, the two Nobel Prizes awarded to Chileans were both for literature. Chile is proudest of its poets, and with good reason. Some of the biggest names in Spanish poetry are from Chile. Considered the first Chilean poem, *La Araucana* is a famous epic piece written at the end of the 16th century by the Spanish soldier and poet Alonso de Ercilla y Zúñiga (1533–1594), who was stationed in Chile. It describes the bravery of the Indians resisting the Spanish conquistadors.

One of the most beloved Chilean poets is Gabriela Mistral (1889–1957), who in 1945 became the first Latin American to be awarded the Nobel Prize for Literature. She was born Lucila Godoy Alcayaga in Vicuña (near La Serena). She was a poor rural schoolteacher who began to write poetry after the man she loved commit suicide. Her poems focus on children, a mother's love (even though she had no children of her own), death, nature and romantic love. Her most distinguished collection of poetry, *Desolación* (Despair), was published in 1922. Her poems are magnificent in their simple treatment of everyday topics, but they can also be dark and complex.

Pablo Neruda (1904–1973), born Neftalí Reyes Basoalto, won the Nobel Prize for Literature in 1971. He is best known and admired for his poetry about love, *Twenty Love Poems and a Song of Despair*, and his celebration of Latin American culture, *Heights of Machu Picchu*. A number of his writings are also political in nature, since he was a devoted communist. Topics include poverty and the plight of the factory worker. He was appointed the Chilean Consul in several countries all across the globe. Neruda died of natural causes in Chile immediately following the 1973 coup. Some say he died from the sadness he felt for his country following the coup.

Well known contemporary Chilean poets include Gonzalo Rojas, Diamela Eltit, Diego Maquieira and Antonio Skármeta. Skármeta is also a fiction writer whose novel, *The Postman*, was made into a successful movie telling the story of Pablo Neruda helping his lovestruck letter-carrier.

Novelists

Jorge Edwards and José Donoso are members of the Latin American 'Boom' (along with Peruvian, Mario Vargas Llosa and Colombian, Gabriel García Márquez). The Boom was a period from the 1960s through the 1980s when a number of Latin American authors wrote internationally acclaimed books. Donoso (1924–1996) was a novelist and short story writer. He often used black humour to tell his stories. Some of his best works are *The Garden Next Door*, *Coronation*, *The Obscene Bird of Night* and *Curfew*.

Jorge Edwards has been a lawyer and foreign service officer, as well as author. He was Deputy Chief of Mission in France when Pablo Neruda was Ambassador. Later he was Chargé d'Affaires in Cuba. His most celebrated book, *Persona Non-Grata*, tells about his experiences in Cuba and being kicked out by Castro. He now dedicates his time to writing and journalism. His fiction has been praised and he has won a number of awards, including the prestigious Cervantes Award.

Isabel Allende, who is a distant cousin of former President Salvador Allende, is one of Latin America's most popular authors. Her most famous work, *The House of Spirits*, is the wonderful story of an eccentric, aristocratic Chilean family. She no longer lives in Chile but the country remains a source of inspiration for her work and she continues to publish critically acclaimed novels.

Ariel Dorfman, novelist and playwright, has achieved worldwide renown for his play *Death and the Maiden*. This story focuses on the confrontation between a torture victim and her tormentor. Dorfman was exiled by the Pinochet government and has been a vocal critic of both this dictatorship and all instances of oppression. Many of his works deal with human rights issues. Luis Sepúlveda's best-known book is *The Old Man Who Read Love Stories*. He does not write travel literature, but his descriptions of South America give you a very precise feeling of what it is like to be there.

Every one of the authors listed earlier—Donoso, Edwards, Allende, Dorfman and Sepúlveda—lived in exile during the

Pinochet government. Some returned to Chile, while others did not. However, following the return to democracy a new wave of authors has popped up on the scene. Alberto Fuguet, Jaime Collyer, Marcela Serrano, Carlos Franz and Ana María del Río, to name just a few, are making major contributions to the Chilean literary tradition.

Condorito

One of Chile's most famous exports to the rest of the Spanish-speaking world is the comic book *Condorito*. It relates the adventures of a character with the head of a condor (the bird of the Andes) who lives in the human world, populated by characters that include his condor-like nephew Coné and his lovely, fully human girlfriend, Yayita.

TRAVEL

Maybe reading one of the authors above has encouraged you to set off and discover other parts of Chile. If you live in Santiago, you owe it to yourself to experience the rest of the country. Chile is so much more than its capital city.

Many Santiaguinos escape to the nearby beaches on weekends.

You need to feel the dry heat of the north, relax amid the lakes and lush forests of the south and suffer the ferocious winds of Patagonia. Travel within Chile is relatively easy and affordable.

Weekend Getaways

If you only have the weekend or don't want to travel too far, there are many places near Santiago worth visiting. Beaches, such as Reñaca, El Quisco, Algarrobo and El Tabo, are the obvious choice, but if you travel a bit further north you'll come upon the coastal towns and beaches of Maitencillo, Zapallar and Papudo. Just off the beach at Cachagua is a big rock that is home to a colony of penguins. Bring your binoculars

Adventure Tourism

Adventure tourism is really taking off in Chile. Some of the most popular activities include: trekking, camping, volcano climbing, mountaineering, glacier crossing, white-water rafting, windsurfing, kayaking, flyfishing, scuba diving, paragliding, bungee jumping, horseback riding, biking and skiing.

to have a look. In line with the conservative nature of the country, there are no topless beaches. This does not mean, however, that you will not see any skimpy bikinis.

A couple of travel companies offer horseback riding tours that begin at the base of the mountains on the outskirts of Santiago. These tours are often a whole day affair and include lunch in the wilderness. Moonlight horseback riding tours (*lunadas*) are also available when there is a full moon.

Wineries can be toured much more extensively than in other wine-producing nations. Chileans will allow you to view every step of the wine making process, which is especially interesting at harvest time. There are many options north, west and south of Santiago, including the Concha y Toro and Santa Rita vineyards.

The Cajón del Maipo, a canyon just south of Santiago, is a nice place to go for a Sunday drive. There are a number of small towns, hostels, nice restaurants and swimming pools. Many people go just to walk and enjoy the fresh air. The Maipo River, which runs through the canyon, offers rafting close to home.

Pomaire, about a 90-minute journey west of Santiago, is known for its clay pottery. This pottery can be found throughout Santiago, but Pomaire offers a better selection, lower prices and a nice getaway for the day. Do not miss the gigantic 1 kg (2 lb) *empanadas*.

There are a number of lakes nearby, the perfect destination for a weekend trip. Rent a cabin or pitch a tent and relax, fish or participate in any number of water sports at Lago Rapel, Lago Vichuquén, Laguna Aculeo, or a bit further to the south, Lago Colbún.

If you prefer to hike, national parks offer acres of beautiful landscape. La Campana, 160 km (100 miles) north of the capital is home to the beautiful Chilean palm tree, which has almost disappeared. You can also climb the challenging La Campana (the Bell) hill. East of Santiago as you head up into the Andes is the Santuario de la Naturaleza. This nature sanctuary is perfect for picnicking, hiking or horseback riding.

The Argentine city of Mendoza lies on the other side of the Andes mountain range. It is a short flight or a five-hour drive from Santiago. If you opt to drive you will experience the quick and intense ascent on the Chilean side and the long slow descent on the bare Argentine side. Crossing the mountains in winter is tricky as many times the border is closed indefinitely due to high snow. Mendoza itself is a very nice town to visit, with lots of shopping, Argentinean wine and restaurants to enjoy.

The North

If you have more time and want to see something different, travel north. This area provides some of the most unique and striking landscapes in Chile. High up in the altiplano in the far north is Lake Chungará. The waters are a beautiful emerald green and the lake is surrounded by volcanoes. You may want to plan your trip to coincide with the La Tirana festival where you can observe the best of Aymara culture. Visit the ghost towns of Isluga, Parinacota and Cosapilla that dot the

As you travel throughout the country, keep a look out for interesting and unique crafts, like these mobiles made out of *totora* (reeds)

landscape. South of Iquique huge pre-Columbian drawings made out of stones adorn the hillsides. It is believed that they were used to guide ancient travellers.

The city of Antofagasta is the stepping off point for many tourist activities in the area. The city itself offers warm water beaches, unlike most of Chile. The Humbolt Current, which originates near Antarctica and flows from south to north,

Old houses, inspired by Victorian and German architecture, are found throughout central and southern Chile.

keeps coastal water temperatures a chilly 15°C (59°F) throughout most of the country. It finally veers out to sea near Antofagasta, making this a perfect place for swimming.

The first place to see is the popular village of San Pedro de Atacama, known for its picturesque colonial church. This town sits on the edge of the driest desert in the world and its archaeological museum has some of the oldest mummies in the world on display. From here you can visit La Valle de la Luna (Valley of the Moon). Due to the type of minerals found here and wind erosion, this strange place gives the illusion of being on the moon. Or, you could go see the flamingos that live in the Flamencos National Reserve. A trip can also be made to the nearby salt flats.

In spite of its severe aridity, every few years the Atacama Desert erupts into a meadow of brightly coloured flowers. If you happen to be in Chile at the time of the Flowering Desert, you could be one of the few people to witness this miracle. Near Lasana you can admire the *Pukara*, fortress-like cities that were built into the hills in the 12th century. Further inland are the Tatio geysers, which come to life at sunrise, spraying steam high up into the air. Further south is the Ojos del Salado Volcano. It is the second highest mountain in the Americas and the highest active volcano in the world.

About five hours north of Santiago lies La Serena. This city offers long beaches and urban entertainment. It is a pleasant place to vacation. From La Serena you can plan a day trip into the stunning Elqui Valley and sample *pisco* at the various distilleries. A short drive to the town of Vicuña will take you to the home and museum of Chile's Nobel laureate, Gabriela Mistral.

Wildlife

Chile's indigenous wildlife include the alpaca, vicuña, llama, guanacos and flamingos found in the altiplano in the north. The Chilean condor lives high up in the Andes mountains. In the south, there are *huemuls* (a large deer) and *pudús* (a small deer), guanacos, *ñandús* (ostrich-like birds) and penguins. A reduced number of pumas roam free in several national parks.

The South

The south of Chile provides a completely different experience. The lush landscape makes it a perfect destination for both traditional and adventure tourists. The Pucón/Villarrica area offers both luxurious hotels and many opportunities for hiking, skiing, etc. In fact, climbing tours will lead you up to the crater of the Villarrica Volcano. You can explore caves and even paraglide. Nearby lakes offer lots of water sports.

Valdivia is a pretty city with a strong German influence. A very interesting museum on Isla Teja houses a beautiful collection of furniture and other items from the days of German immigration. Many tourists travel here to explore the forts built by the Spanish at Corral, Niebla and Isla Mancera. The fortresses date from the 17th century and were built at the mouth of the Calle Calle River, which links the Pacific Ocean to Valdivia. Boats travel between the three forts and you are encouraged to roam about at your own pace.

The south is also known for its hot springs. One of the most famous places to relax and benefit from the waters is at the Hotel Termas Puyehue, near Puyehue National Park. In addition to enjoying the hot springs, guests can enjoy a number of outdoor activities, such as hiking, horseback riding or skiing. The hotel sits on the shores of Lake Puyehue and the volcano of the same name rises above nearby. For those with a lot of time, the road continues up and over the Andes and leads you into Argentina and the stunning city of San Carlos de Bariloche.

The Lake District is known for its beautiful lakes, volcanoes, hot springs and forests. Frutillar is a quaint town on the shores of Lake Llanquihue (meaning deep place). There are places to spend the night and lots of restaurants, especially German ones. On the shores of the same lake lies the tranquil town of Puerto Varas. Here, as well as in Frutillar, you can enjoy views of the Osorno Volcano. Puerto Varas offers everything from luxurious to budget lodging. Tours will take you behind the volcano to the Saltos de Petrohué. Here the waters rush over volcanic rock. Further down the road is the emerald green Lago

> **Flora**
>
> There are thousands of unique plant species in Chile. The copihue, which is found in southern Chile, is the national flower. It is a vine from the lily family that produces a red, white or pink bell-shaped flower. The alerce tree, a slow-growing tree found in the south, is noted for its longevity. Some alerces are over 4,000 years old. Because the wood is water resistant, many homes in the region are made from these trees and sadly many forests have been depleted. The government is trying to preserve what is left for future generations. Another beautiful tree seen throughout the central and south central regions is the large and stately araucaria tree, called a monkey puzzle tree in English. At times you may hear indigenous groups referred to as Araucanos, a term derived from the tree native to their homeland.

Todos los Santos located in the Vicente Peréz Rosales National Park. Boats take you on an afternoon cruise to a hotel on the other side and you have the option of eating lunch before returning, staying the night, or continuing on to Argentina through a series of bus and boat rides.

Puerto Montt is the largest city in the Lake District. It sits on the Reloncaví Inlet. This modern city serves as the beginning of the Carretera Austral, the gateway to the island of Chiloé and the port for cruises to the Laguna San Rafael. The Carretera Austral (Southern Highway) is primarily a gravel road that takes you south to Coyhaique and beyond. The road is long and difficult but provides spectacular views. This area is extremely isolated and if you are brave enough to attempt the drive, make sure you have stockpiles of gasoline and food because you will not find many supplies along the route.

The San Rafael Lagoon is a lake at the tip of a fjord which boasts a magnificent glacier. When you arrive, the lake is dotted with small boats, full of tourists drinking whiskey 'on the rocks', i.e., poured over million-year-old pieces of ice from the glacier. The cruises range from barebones to the luxurious and depending upon the itinerary, may take as little as two days to reach the Laguna. The more expensive cruises make a number of stops at picturesque fishing towns and hot springs along the way, stretching out the experience.

Natural Beauty

CONAF, the National Forest Corporation, administers 32 national parks, 48 national reserves and 15 natural monuments. Below is a list of some of the most notable. Nominal entrance fees.

- Lauca National Park—Lake Chungará
- La Campana National Park—One of last remaining Chilean palm forests
- Conguillío National Park—Llaima volcano and Araucaria (monkey-puzzle tree) forest
- Alerce Andino National Park—Alerce forest (enormous, ancient, slow-growing larch trees)
- Fray Jorge Forest National Park—Lush forest in the midst of an arid region due to the camanchaca (coastal mist)
- Laguna San Rafael National Park—Get up close to the Mount San Valentín glacier
- Villarrica National Park—Volcano Villarrica (hike up to the crater, ski)
- Rio Simpson National Reserve—Fly fishing on the Simpson River
- Radal Siete Tazas National Reserve—Seven waterfalls that spill into seven little pools or 'cups'
- Rapa Nui National Park—Easter Island culture, Moais
- Juan Fernández Archipelago National Park—Robinson Crusoe Island
- Los Flamencos National Reserve—Flamingos, salt deposits, Moon Valley
- Vicente Pérez Rosales National Park—Osorno Volcano, Todos Los Santos Lake, Petrohué waterfalls
- Pumalín Park—The largest private park in the world at 720,000 acres. The land was purchased by American Douglas Tompkins in 1991 in order to protect it. It is open to the public with no admission fee.

Chilean Patagonia

Punta Arenas is the beginning point for any trip to Torres del Paine, the cave of the *milodón* or the penguin colony at Otway Inlet. The *milodón* is a large, sloth like animal that is now extinct. Skin and other remains of this legendary animal were found in this cave. Today, a large statue of a *milodon* is the only thing to welcome you to the cave. Tours to all of the local attractions can be arranged in Santiago or from Punta Arenas. One of the most spectacular locations in all of Chile is the Torres del Paine National Park, named a Biosphere Reserve by UNESCO in 1978. The park offers amazing scenery and is filled with a variety of plants and wild animals, such as *ñandues* and *guanacos*. The most striking feature is the granite towers known as the Cuernos (or the Horns).

Part of the reason this park remains unspoiled is because of the modest amount of infrastructure. To really experience this park and see the glaciers, lakes, rivers, mountains and waterfalls, you should do some hiking. A hiking trail circles the park, but it can only be completed during the summer months by knowledgeable hikers. There are designated areas for pitching tents (be careful, sometimes the wind is so strong that it systematically and repeatedly uproots the tents). For the very adventurous, there is glacier crossing, climbing and kayaking. Many of those who do not want to rough it, chose to stay in a shelter (*refugio*) or hotel (ranging from simple to five-star) and make day trips. *Refugios*, spread throughout the park, are small wooden huts with a couple of bunk rooms, a common area and a kitchen. You can pay to have the cook make you a meal, or you can prepare your own food that you brought with you. The bunkbeds are bare, so you need to supply your own sleeping bag.

International Travel

Living in Santiago makes it easier to travel to Latin America's most popular destinations. There are regular flights to Rio de Janeiro, Lima and Buenos Aires, among other cities. Or, plan a trip to see the ruins of Machu Picchu in Peru. Travel agents in Santiago can help you plan your trip and provide information on the necessary paperwork.

Accommodations

Throughout Chile you can find accommodations for all budgets. At the lower end are *hospedajes*, which are family homes with rooms for rent that normally include breakfast and a shared bathroom and sitting room. *Residencias* or *residenciales* are small hotels and *pensiones* offer a private bath. If travelling to the beach or a lake, *cabañas* (cabins) are a good option. At the top are hotels, both modest and luxurious. Many travel agencies in Santiago sell package tours for those who prefer the convenience.

Transportation

Trains in Chile tend to be slow and old, but are in the process of being upgraded, particularly along the Santiago-Concepción corridor. Better options are to either fly or take a bus. There are a number of different bus classes. For long or overnight rides, the most expensive class offers wide seats that recline well over 45 degrees. The ride is very pleasant and is much cheaper than plane fare. The ticket includes beverages (both alcoholic and non-alcoholic), dinner and breakfast. There is a bus attendant who fulfils your every need and organises games for the passengers. Movies are also shown on board. These buses normally leave in the evening and arrive early morning and surprisingly you arrive refreshed and ready to take on the day. *Buen viaje!*

SPORTS

As mentioned above, many extreme sports are becoming popular in Chile. If you are not a risk taker, you can enjoy a number of traditional sports, although in general, Chile is not a sports-crazed society.

Soccer

Soccer (called *fútbol* in Spanish) is undoubtedly the most common sport in Chile, or Latin America for that matter. Almost every child learns how to play soccer and will continue to play into adulthood. On weekends, organised and informal soccer games are played throughout the country. One reason why soccer is so popular is because everyone can play regardless of income level. The game does not require expensive equipment, a ball and empty field will do.

Every city or mid-sized town has at least one professional soccer team. Chile is not one of the big names like Argentina or Brazil; nevertheless, the level of play is very high. However, there is a large gap between the big clubs who pay their players very high salaries and have great facilities and the

smaller clubs that have much tighter budgets. The biggest teams are Colo Colo, Catholic University and University of Chile. Marcelo 'Matador' Salas and Iván 'Bam Bam' Zamorano are local and international heroes. Matías Fernández is the big newcomer.

Soccer games are indeed an event, complete with fireworks and giant flags. Chilean soccer fans are very enthusiastic and the stadiums are full an hour and a half before the game. While there is no major gang problem in Chile, some gangs have formed among soccer supporters. At games the fans wear the colours of their team and sit in specific sections of the stadium. You should be aware that fights and violence can erupt when fierce rivals play one another. Do not be surprised to see lots of policemen at a soccer game. The official soccer season runs from March through December with two major championships—the Opening Championship (Campeonato de Apetura) and the Official Championship. Matches are usually held on Saturday and Sunday, occasionally on Wednesday, generally at 4:00 pm.

Tennis

Chileans enjoy other sports as well, although their cost is prohibitive for many. Sports such as polo, rugby, golf and

Although many have the impression that cockfighting is popular in Latin America, it is illegal in Chile and not common. The same applies to bull fighting which was banned in the 19th century.

tennis are generally reserved for the upper classes. Tennis is a favourite spectator sport because from time to time Chile produces top rate players. Anita Lizana won the US Open Championship in 1937. Patricio Cornejo, Hans Gildemeister and Jaime Fillol were great in the 1980's. Marcelo 'El Chino' Ríos was a top-seeded men's player in the 1990's. Nicolás 'Vampiro' Massú and Fernando González are internationally competitive players today.

Horses

Chile has fine horseback riders, as there is a large enough upper class to support the sport, and the national team usually does well at the Olympics. A Chilean rider, Alberto Larraguibel (now deceased) holds the international high jumping record for horses.

Horse racing is a more popular spectator sport, with fine Chilean horses appearing at tracks around the world. The two main racing events each year are the Derby in Viña del Mar in January and El Ensayo in Santiago in October.

Kayaking and other outdoor sports allow you to enjoy the beautiful Chilean landscape.

Basketball

Basketball is popular in southern Chile because it can be played indoors during the long, wet winter. There is a professional league, with players imported from other countries. You can follow the sport at http://www.latinbasket.com/chi/chi.asp. The Chileans generally do well at Latin American basketball tournaments.

Skiing and Snowboarding

Skiing is a popular sport in Chile among the wealthy. There are a number of ski resorts just outside of Santiago, making it easy to ski on weekends. Their location also makes it convenient for international tourists, who can fly to Santiago to ski when it is summer in the northern hemisphere. Skiing in Chile offers challenging slopes that are well groomed with good chairlifts. Most ski resorts are above the tree line and offer a unique panorama. Some resorts even have a sea view! Ski season is from June to September or October. There are 16 ski centres in Chile, most found between Santiago and Osorno. The most important resorts are Portillo, 160 km (100 miles) from Santiago, and the Farellones-La Parva-Valle Nevado-El Colorado complex only 50 km (31 miles) away, high up in the mountains.

CHILDREN'S GAMES

If your children have Chilean friends or attend a Chilean school you may be surprised by the new games they learn. Of course, Chilean children play many games that are common to all cultures, such as *bolitas* (marbles), *luche* (hopscotch), *escondida* (hide and go seek), *pillarse* (tag), checkers, jump rope, roller skates and kites, and assorted video games. *Rayuela*, popular in the countryside, is a coin pitch game that originated in Spain. Disks or coins are thrown to a line drawn on the ground. The player who gets closest to the line wins the other players' coins. Little kids will enjoy a run-run, a makeshift toy made by passing thread through the holes of a large button and twisting it. Pull the ends, and the button spins.

LANGUAGE

CHAPTER 8

'What a good language mine is, what a good tongue we
inherited from the harsh conquistadors... We ended up
losing...we ended up winning...They took the gold and they
left us the gold...They took everything and they left
us everything... they left us their words.'
—Pablo Neruda, *Confieso que he vivido: memorias*

THE OFFICIAL LANGUAGE of Chile is Spanish, the language brought by the *conquistadors* several hundred years ago. Despite the time and distance, Spanish spoken in Latin America is remarkably similar to the Spanish spoken in Spain. There are many more pronunciation and vocabulary differences between the English spoken in the US and England. As a result, all Spanish speakers can communicate with one another quite easily.

Having said that, the Chilean accent is one of the most difficult accents to understand for students of Spanish. In fact, many Chileans readily admit that theirs is not the prettiest Spanish. Often it sounds like the speaker is mumbling as letters and sounds are dropped and words are mashed together. Add to this the words borrowed from the indigenous peoples and the slang that Chileans love to use and learning to speak Spanish in Chile can become quite trying. But, bear with it and eventually you'll be able to understand what is being said to you and you might even catch yourself starting to speak as the Chileans do.

Speaking Spanish

When Susan first arrived in Chile, having studied Spanish for over four years, she became frustrated and dismayed when she was unable to understand the Chileans she was meeting. She started to believe that all the effort she had put into learning Spanish had been an utter waste of time. Only when she heard an interview on the news with the President of Mexico and was able to understand him did she realise that it was the Chilean accent, not her, that had made everything so difficult.

> ### Chilean Spanish
> The terms *español* and *castellano* are equivalents in describing the language of Chile, but *castellano* is used more frequently. It does not refer to any language specific to the Castile region of Spain (near Toledo), as the name implies, rather it is a derivation of the word for the Spanish language that pays homage to the historic importance of the kingdom of Castile in the formation of the modern Spanish state. So don't worry that you may learn some deviant type of Spanish in Chile. Throughout South America, *castellano* is the word used for Spanish. *Español* is more common in Central and North America.

PRONUNCIATION

Regional differences in the language of the Chilean people are remarkably slight, despite the country's varied geography and great length. Chilean Spanish is generally the same from north to south, a result of the fact that the Spaniards settled in a small area in the centre of the country and migrated slowly and in small numbers to the north and

the south. Today, television and radio help to homogenise Chilean Spanish. There are, however, noticeable differences in accents, usually based on socio-economic background. As in most countries, the upper classes and the educated speak a more refined language than the lower classes.

Pronunciation Guide:

The 'd' is lost in the endings -ado and -ido: hablao (*hablado*)

The 'd' is almost lost in the endings -ad and -ud: verdá (*verdad*), salú (*salud*).

The intervocalic 'd' is almost lost: deo (*dedo*), náa (*nada*).

The intervocalic 'r' is weak: páa (*para*).

The omission of the intervocalic 'g' is considered vulgar: juar (*jugar*).

The 's' may be pronounced completely (*asno*), aspirated (*ahno*), assimilated (*anno*) or completely omitted (*fóforo*).

The 'ch' may be more fricative, or similar to the 'sh' sound. For example: *Shile, Pinoshet*. However, this is considered to be a sign of a lack of culture.

Chileans tend to put in a rolled 'r' sound before certain words that they would like to emphasise—Rrrrrr—*bueno*.

A large part of what gives foreigners that foreign sound in Spanish is the pronunciation of a sentence. The individual words are often pronounced well, but that is precisely the error. It is the nature of Spanish to start every syllable with a consonant, thereby frequently linking one word with the next. For example, "*Los amigos aman a las Ariqueñas*" will be pronounced in everyday speech like this: "*Lo sa mi go sa ma na la sa ri que ñas.*" Listen to Chileans in natural conversation to get a feel for this. Our best advice on picking up a good accent is to study intently the lips and tongue position and to imitate it. It takes training to make your mouth take these shapes. An English accent in Chile has been compared to talking with a hot potato in one's mouth. Laura remembers that her mouth ached when she started to learn Spanish in earnest. But realistically, anyone who learns a language after puberty will have some trace of an accent.

Simple pleasures like buying ice cream will require some knowledge of Spanish

VOCABULARY

One must be very careful when imitating the colloquial vocabulary in any country. Native speakers have much more leeway when it comes to using popular speech, which often sounds silly or insulting coming from foreigners. This applies especially to vulgar words. It is easy to pick up bad words, not always knowing what they mean literally, but knowing when they are used. It is best to try to find more elegant terminology to express your sentiments. Be sure to ask the Chileans about their slang and pronunciations, as they love to explain them to visitors.

The following are some highlights of Chilean slang:

Chilean Slang	English Meaning
Ahuasado	naive or a shy person (comes from *huaso* meaning a country bumpkin or cowboy). This is somewhat of an insult to *huasos*, even though the term *huaso* itself has no negative connotation

Chilean Slang	English Meaning
al tiro	quickly
Bachichas	Italians
Beatle	turtleneck (in deference to the Fab Four)
cabros	kids
cachai?	"Get it?" added to the end of many sentences
cacharro	auto
cachureo	junk, things of low value
cartera	purse (not wallet as in other Spanish-speaking countries)
Coños	Spaniards, called so because of how often the Spanish use this offensive expletive
cuico/a	a conservative person, generally of a socio-economic class above one's own, a snob, someone who flaunts his/her wealth
chaleco	cardigan or vest
Ches	Argentineans
Cholos	Peruvians or Bolivians, also a degrading term for Indians
choro	an exclamation similar to cool!
choreado	to be infuriated or bored.
chomba or chompa	sweater
chupamedias or patero	someone who sucks up to his/her boss
darse vuelta la chaqueta	to change political affiliation
dije	nice
es lo que hay	what you see is what you get, has a negative tone.
falluto or chueco	one who is not always correct

Chilean Slang	English Meaning
fome	boring
Gabachos	French
gallo	a guy, a man
la gallada	the people
gringos	Americans and Britons
gordo/a	term of endearment, literally fat or fatty
guagua	baby
harto	1) adjective—a lot, plenty; 2) verb—*estar harto/a*—to be fed up, unable to stand or support something anymore
huevón/ona (noun.& adjective)	can be a vulgar expression or an affectionate chiding. To say this while holding one hand palm up, fingers curled, as if holding an apple, is a very obscene and insulting gesture.
lolo/a	teenager
luca	1,000 (commonly used to refer to 1,000 pesos)
mina	woman
mono	a monkey; a cartoon; a doodle, depending on the context.
negro/a	a term of endearment
onda	the essence or spirit of something, often used in the expression *Qué onda?* meaning What's up? or What's your problem?
oye!	an informal greeting, roughly the equivalent of "hey," but much more widespread
pacos	police officers
palta	Chilean for avocado

Chilean Slang	English Meaning
palta reina	stuffed avocado, usually with tuna
patrona	wife, which shows who has the power in the Chilean family!
pega	work
peinando la muñeca	literally "combing the doll's hair", meaning mentally disturbed
pelados	members of the army (because of their short haircuts), also a term of endearment for babies
pelusas	poor children
pesado/a	an obnoxious person or a party pooper
pinchar	to win someone over, or score (i.e. with a woman or man)
pico	although this word is widely used in many other countries, meaning a little, in Chile it is slang for penis
pituto	a contact who can arrange for special treatment or privileges
plop!	an interjection which expresses surprise or bewilderment, taken from the Chilean comic strip *Condorito*
polera	T-shirt
pololear	to go steady, to have a serious romantic relationship with someone
pololo/a	boyfriend/girlfriend
por si acaso	just in case or by the way. In Chile, and much of the Spanish-speaking world, the slang use of this is *por si las moscas*
puh/po	an abbreviated form of *pues*, used to add emphasis, generally at the end of a sentence. e.g. *Si poh! No poh!*

Chilean Slang	English Meaning
rasca	in bad taste, tacky, of bad quality or poorly made; or a low-class person or someone without manners
regalón/ona	the pet or favourite person, one that is spoiled or pampered
regalonear	to pamper
regio	super, great, excellent
rico	excellent, good, referring to food or drink, or an attractive, sexy person
roto/picante	an unrefined person
salvaje	an upper-class (cuico) term meaning great
si po'	an abbreviated form of si pues, yes or of course
sinvergüenza	a person who is unafraid to say what he/she thinks; a crook
suche	lowly worker
taco	traffic jam or the heel of a shoe
Te fijas?/Te fijai?	Get it? Did you understand?
tintolio	red wine
tucada	great sum of money

OTHER LANGUAGE CONSIDERATIONS
Voseo

If you have studied Spanish formally, you may remember the informal second person plural form is *vosotros*. We say 'may' because many textbooks omit the form completely, since, for the most part, it is not used by the great majority of Spanish speakers. In Chile *voseo* may be considered a sign of poor education. While the textbooks claim it is the second person plural, most people use it as the informal singular, in other words, replacing the *tú* form with the *vosotros* form. For example *Cómo estáis?* Or, in Chile, the abbreviated *Cómo estái?*, a common expression when talking to one person, when theoretically it should be used for more than one person. You may also hear people substitute the subject pronoun *vos* for *tú*, another phenomenon common throughout Latin America. Do note that even though the speaker uses the subject pronoun *vos*, the indirect and direct object pronoun is still *te* and the possessive forms are still *tu* and *tuyo*. For example, *Vos quédate aquí!*, *Vas vos en tu auto?* However, substituting *vos* for *tú* in Chile is a sign of poor education, unlike in other Latin American countries where its use is widespread.

Kiosks offer every type of reading material, from newspapers to gossip magazines, to help you practice your Spanish.

Tú versus Usted

One aspect of the Spanish language that makes it different from the English language is the division of pronouns into formal or informal. Every person you speak with must be classified into one or the other category. This is a tough call for many foreigners in Chile, especially native English speakers, who are not used to making the distinction. Many people have the mistaken notion that it would be better to use the informal term with everyone, but this is not the true nature of the Spanish language. In general, native speakers probably use *Usted* much more than *tú* once they leave their houses. Unless you marry a Chilean or have many intimate friends, the formal form will be much more important to you.

Usted is actually an abbreviation of *Vuestra Merced*, roughly translated as Your Grace, a title used in Spain hundreds of years ago. It is important to remember that *Usted* is the norm and *tú* is a privilege only granted to certain individuals. *Usted* is used with guests, older people, anyone in a position of authority, or anyone you do not know. *Usted* is always used in business relationships, even if the social status is the same.

You may have known your secretary, boss or colleague for many years, but the relationship will almost always be on an *Usted* basis. Even among family members *Usted* can be heard, especially with distant relatives, when there is a large age gap between family members, or with relatives by marriage. Parents often use the *Usted* form with their children as a term of endearment.

With people of your own age and status whom you meet in a social setting you will probably start off using *tú*. It is recommended that you follow the lead of Chileans until you are able to judge for yourself. The change from *Usted* to *tú* can happen quickly, and marks the recognition of a certain intimacy in the relationship.

In some cases one person may use *Usted*, while the other uses *tú*. This may happen when adults speak to children (or between any two people with a large age gap—be careful not to offend an older person by using *tú* with

them in response to their use of *tú* with you!), or when servants speak to employers and vice versa. To use a famous example, Don Quixote used *tú* when speaking with Sancho Panza, his manservant, but Sancho always used *Vuestra Merced* with Don Quixote, his master. This example is of course from 17th century Spanish literature, but the principle is still valid in Chile today.

The term *Don* comes from the phrase *De Origen Noble* (of noble origin). It replaces the title *Señor*. Today in Chile the terms *Don* and *Doña* (for women) are used to show respect. Placed before the person's first name, they are often used to show extreme respect when addressing someone with a remarkably important position, such as ambassador, minister or other high offices. Though it reflects a level of intimacy, it would be perfectly acceptable to address, for example, former President Lagos as Don Ricardo. It is also used to show respect even if social status is not that different. *Empleadas* and *nanas* always address their male employers as *Don* and female employers as *Doña* or *Señora*. If the *empleada* is older, she will, in turn, be addressed as *Doña* or *Señora*. An office worker may use *Don* to address a boss. Similarly, the junior (a male employee responsible for miscellaneous errands), although from a lower social standing, will be addressed as *Don* if he is older. Use of the term is linked to the use of *Usted*. No matter how close these relationships become, as a sign of respect, the informal *tú* will never be used. Chileans, no matter what their social level, would never refer to themselves as *Don* or Doña, as this would seem presumptuous.

About Friends

Chileans, as do others in the Southern Cone of South America, use the article *la* or *el* before a name when talking about someone they know personally. For example, if talking about Carmen, a friend who is not present, you would say: "*La Carmen vendrá mañana*", as opposed to just "*Carmen vendrá mañana*". (Carmen will come tomorrow.) When listing people as part of an informal conversation, you would say: "*el Manuel, la Luisa, el Pedro*, etc."

Always use the formal *Usted* (you) when addressing people in the service industry.

DOING BUSINESS

'Born under the sign of poverty, the country learned that it should be sober, extremely hard-working and maintain civil peace because of its scant resources and limited population.'
—Gabriela Mistral, *Breve Descripción de Chile*

THE ECONOMY

Chile is often referred to as the star of Latin America in terms of its economic performance and Chileans do have a right to be proud. In the wake of free-market reforms that promoted non-traditional industries, foreign trade and privatisation, Chile is one of the fastest growing economies in Latin America. GDP growth has been steady and impressive and the country currently enjoys a trade surplus. Foreign debt is being paid down and remains low by Latin American standards. Inflation has been reduced, hovering between 2 and 4 per cent, and the unemployment rate is relatively low.

Chile's geographical location has always contributed to the isolation of the country. This remoteness has greatly affected its economy as well as other aspects of Chilean life. Prior to the late 1970s, the market had been closed. The country was dependent on one single export product—copper. However, the change over the past decades has been drastic. Chile now exports thousands of products, which are gaining recognition the world over. And on the flip side, Chileans now have access to a wider array of consumer goods. The country is more affluent than ever before. Unfortunately, while Chileans in general are doing better, poverty still affects about 18 per cent of the population and the gap between the 'haves' and the 'have-nots' is widening. In fact, it is one of the most severe in all of Latin America.

A BRIEF HISTORY

Like most Latin American countries during the 1940–1960s, Chile practiced Import-Substitution Industrialisation (ISI). The goal of ISI was to free the country from dependence on foreign economies through domestic or regional industrialisation. Production took place within the country's borders and high tariffs and non-tariff barriers were erected to protect these struggling industries. Chilean products faced very little competition since imports were severely restricted. The end result was inefficiency and high prices.

Socialism

The struggling economy came to a virtual standstill following the election of Salvador Allende, a socialist, in 1970. A combination of many factors, primarily bad policies combined with international and domestic sabotage, led to the ruin of the economy. Allende nationalised a great many industries and his populist policies such as price controls led to shortages. The situation was aggravated by the large amount of factory takeovers by the workers, which reduced overall productivity. Inflation spiralled out of control and a black market emerged. A series of strikes and the cessation of international investment sealed the economy's fate.

The Military Government and Free-Market Reforms

The military regime that ousted Allende in a coup in 1973 immediately focused on the economy. In the mid-1970s, the Pinochet government, advised by a number of technocrats educated at the University of Chicago known as the 'Chicago Boys', implemented a process of rapid economic liberalisation. Tariffs were reduced and non-tariff barriers were eliminated. The strategy was to make domestic production more efficient as Chilean firms faced an influx of imports. The government also sought to diversify the economy, eliminating the country's dependence on copper. A series of privatisations were initiated and the role of the state was severely reduced. Labor unions were outlawed and any manner of dissent or protest was repressed. Workers were effectively and harshly prevented from bargaining or demonstrating to improve wages or working conditions, which had sunk drastically. A number of Chilean firms went bankrupt in the face of stiff international competition, which led to further hardship when their employees lost their jobs. Unemployment increased dramatically and the number of Chileans living below the poverty line rose to over 40 per cent. In 1983 the economy fell into a deep recession. It took over three years for the country to recover.

Many analysts credit the military government with saving the Chilean economy. However, it should not be overlooked that the wealthy got wealthier while many Chileans fell deep into poverty with no means of escaping. Furthermore, academics continue to debate to this day whether these severe economic reforms could have been carried out under a democratic government responsible to the electorate.

Current Economy

By the time a democratic government was elected to power in 1990, the economy was strong. Subsequent democratic governments have continued with essentially the same economic policies instituted by the military regime. However, this has been done in accordance with a wide array of social policies and programmes, and labour unions were once again legalised. The greatest consequence of these policies has been the radical reduction in the number of Chileans living below the poverty line

REGIONAL TRADE AGREEMENTS

The Chilean economy is export led. Non-traditional products have garnered respect throughout the world for their high quality, especially Chilean wine, fruit, vegetables, paper and seafood. Roughly one-third of Chilean products are exported to Asia, one-third to the European Community and the other third throughout the Americas (slightly more than half to other Latin American countries and the remainder going to North America). When looked at individually, the United States is the number one recipient of Chilean exports. Yet,

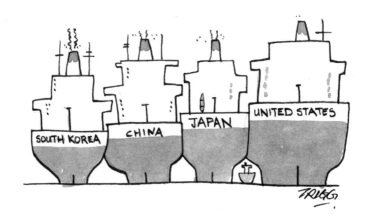

the significance of Asia cannot be ignored. Japan, China and South Korea are second, third and fourth in terms of export markets. This strategy of promoting exports across the globe lessens Chilean dependence on one trading partner.

Recognising the undeniable importance of free trade, Chile has entered into a large number of free trade agreements. Chile signed a free trade agreement with MERCOSUR, the South American Customs Union comprised of Argentina, Brazil, Paraguay and Uruguay. It also signed separate free trade agreements with Canada, Mexico, Colombia, Venezuela, Ecuador, Peru, Bolivia, some Central American countries and the European Union. After long negotiations, Chile has a free trade agreement with the United States. In Asia, Chile has free trade agreements with China, South Korea, Singapore and Japan and is in negotiations with India. Chile is a member of APEC (Asia-Pacific Economic Cooperation) and PECC (Pacific Economic Cooperation Council). For those countries that do not have a free trade agreement with Chile there is a uniform tariff rate of 6 per cent on all imported items.

EXPORTS

A large part of Chile's success can be attributed to the diversification of its exports. At one point, copper sales made up 80 per cent of the country's exports. That figure has dropped to 45 per cent in 2005. Chile has turned to the strengths of its distinct regions, each of which makes a

A high percentage of Chilean exports pass through Valparaíso, one of the country's principle ports.

significant contribution to the Chilean economy. The north is the heart of the mining industry and the Central Valley is famous for its wines and agricultural produce. Forestry, fishing and tourism bring in dollars in the south. As a result, Chile now exports more than 3,400 distinct products. Some of the most important sectors of the economy are listed below.

Mining

Mining was and continues to be a fundamental component of the Chilean economy. Nitrate deposits in the northern regions were big business during the second half of the nineteenth century, so much so that it was called 'white gold'. At its height, there were over 60 mines in the Atacama Desert with 15,000 workers. However, synthetic nitrates invented by the Germans during World War I offered a cheap alternative and soon the desert was littered with abandoned mines and ghost towns. Fortunately, nitrate was not the only valuable mineral in the northern desert. Chile has the world's largest reserves of copper (around one-quarter of global supplies) and is the number one exporter of copper in the world. Chile has the second largest reserves of lithium, substantial reserves of iron, silver, salt, zinc, manganese, molybdenum, gold, coal, iodine and moderate reserves of oil and natural gas in the extreme south.

Service Sector
The service sector accounts for a huge percentage of GDP. One of the fastest growing sectors, it encompasses a vast number of areas including financial services (banking, securities, asset management, insurance, etc.), professional services (accounting, legal, engineering, consulting, architecture, etc.), commerce, utilities, construction, communication, informatics, transportation, housing, education, health, tourism and public administration.

Agriculture
Farming and agro-industries play a major role in the economy. Chile grows a wide variety of fruits and vegetables for export. Fresh and processed fruits and vegetables account for more than 70 per cent of total agricultural exports. Chilean produce has a ready market during the winter season in the northern hemisphere. These products include grapes, apples, pears, kiwis, plums, nectarines, peaches, asparagus, tomatoes and corn. In fact, Chile is the world's second largest exporter of table grapes after Italy.

Poisoned Grapes
In 1989, an anonymous tip-off alerted US officials at the American Embassy in Santiago that grapes in a large shipment originating in Chile had been poisoned with cyanide. The US immediately suspended all imports of grapes, as did many other countries. The Chilean economy suffered greatly as a result. Citing procedural errors in the US government lab that had run the tests on the grapes, the Chilean government and private Chilean companies demanded compensation from the US government. The case, which was viewed as a threat to the Pinochet government, has never been fully resolved.

Forestry

The forestry sector is vital to the Chilean economy. Forty-five per cent of the land is suitable for forestry and 13.4 million hectares are covered by native forests. However, most of the industry uses plantations. The majority of trees cultivated are Radiata pine and eucalyptus because they grow significantly faster in Chile than in other countries. Chile is among the world's largest exporters of cellulose acetate. Other principal wood exports are pulp, chips, sawn wood and paper.

Wines

Chilean wines now hold a prominent place on the global market. They have a strong reputation as good quality wines at affordable prices. Chile's distinct geography has proven useful to the wine industry. The sea to the west and the Andes Mountains to the east have protected the vines from foreign insects and diseases. In fact, the Andes protected Chilean vineyards from phylloxera, a disease that had severely damaged the wine industry in Europe. Making news around the globe, the Carmenére grape that was thought to have been wiped out in France, was later found misidentified in Chile. This delicious wine is now being produced in Chile to great reviews.

Fishing

One of the most dynamic sectors of the Chilean economy has been the fishing industry. Due to the cold waters of the Pacific Ocean coming up from Antarctica, Chile is an optimal place for a wide variety of fish and seafood. The development of salmon farms has been especially impressive. Chile began exporting salmon in 1984 and in only 10 years rose to be the second largest exporter of salmon in the world behind Norway. Other products include trout, hake, cod, conger eel, sea bass, swordfish, abalone, sea urchin, scallops, octopus, shrimp and crabs. Chile is also the largest exporter of fishmeal in the world.

Energy

One area of concern is the energy sector. Chile urgently needs to expand the availability of energy sources in order to be able to continue fueling the expansion of the economy. The country depends heavily on hydroelectric energy because it produces small amounts of oil and gas. The importation of natural gas has been only partially successful. Other options, such as geothermal and solar energy or a revival of the coal industry will probably have to be considered. There is strong opposition to the use of nuclear energy.

FOREIGN INVESTMENT

Chile receives the highest level of foreign investment as a percentage of GDP in all of Latin America. Top investors are the US, Canada, Finland, the United Kingdom, Japan, Spain and Australia. The main beneficiary of foreign capital is the mining sector. The infrastructure, energy, telecommunications and forestry industries also receive significant amounts of foreign capital. Some foreign businesses undertake a public works project as a concession, and recoup their investment through user fees collected during the length of the contract.

Many multinational corporations choose to set up their Latin American headquarters in Santiago because of low costs, a highly educated workforce, high quality infrastructure, transparency in the regulatory system and expertise in regional distribution and logistics. Chile was ranked the most competitive nation in the region, even higher than some European nations, in the 2006 Global Competitiveness Report. Furthermore, foreign investors are treated the same as Chilean investors.

This rise in foreign investment has been accompanied by a change in attitude. Foreign capital is now seen as a business partner in the country's development. This is a drastic change from the 1960s when the predominant view was that multi-national corporations served only to strip the country of its wealth without stimulating further development.

Investment Abroad

Not only does Chile receive a great deal of foreign capital, but Chilean firms themselves are also investing abroad. A majority of investments have been made in Argentina. Chilean firms also have interests in Peru, Bolivia, Brazil and Ecuador. Chilean corporations are investing in sectors such as banking, insurance, supermarkets, electricity distribution, telecommunications, computer software and

The explosive growth of the Chilean economy is reflected in the dramatic increase of new construction.

the manufacturing of cookies and candy. Chile also provides 'technical exports', i.e., the transfer of knowledge and expertise. Chileans boast about the fact that their pension and health care systems have been studied carefully by several other countries. Chilean assistance has been provided in designing and setting up similar systems elsewhere.

GENERAL BUSINESS CLIMATE

Working in Chile will present some minor challenges, although the government makes every attempt to aid foreign investors. It promotes an open economy, keeps the level of state intervention to a minimum and strongly encourages free enterprise. A slew of government publications are available detailing start-up requirements, special trade zones, accounting requirements, corporate taxes, exchange rates, etc. Furthermore, CORFO (Chilean Economic Development Agency) and Cinver (Chilean Foreign Investment Committee) provide significant help in setting up a business in Chile.

Useful Websites

CORFO : http://www.corfo.cl

Cinver: http://www.cinver.cl

While multi-national corporations are routinely welcomed to Chile, they could face be a bit of opposition from some sectors of society. For example, few Chileans would like to see the copper industry back in the hands of foreign companies, if only for nationalistic reasons. Furthermore, the growing environmental movement has a somewhat negative opinion of international companies. Some Chileans allege that these corporations, having destroyed their own homelands, are now pillaging the lands of the Third World.

Doing Business

The following section focuses on the general office environment in Chile. However, many people who have been posted to Chile will not find themselves behind a desk, especially those working in the mining, fishing and forestry industries. All in all, those who work in these fields may find a more relaxed working atmosphere. Moreover, in industries that have high levels of foreign investment, the expatriate may be working with Chileans who have had much more

Many Chilean and international companies have located their offices in the El Bosque neighbourhood of Las Condes.

direct experience with foreigners. Each industry is unique and because foreigners are involved in widely differing sectors from finance to hospitality to infrastructure, this section can provide only sweeping generalisations.

Cultural Differences

In general, those who work in a branch office of a multinational corporation will encounter an overall work ethic close to that of the parent country. Nevertheless, when dealing with Chileans, either as clients or employees, even minor cultural differences must be taken into consideration. The most obvious differences are summarised below.

Business Meetings

Chileans tend to conduct their business affairs in the office. Unlike in many other countries where a major business deal is hammered out over an extended lunch, on the golf course or at a nightclub, Chileans close the deal in a formal business setting. It is very important to reconfirm any meeting or appointment prior to the actual date.

Most offices have more than one telephone number. This is a holdover from the days when it was cheaper to add another line than to install a switchboard. Calling any of the numbers listed will put you in contact with the receptionist. It is also common practice in Chile for the secretary to screen and place most of her boss's calls. In the past, callers were attended to rather quickly, but today, with the sharp increase in business activity, people tend to be left on hold more often and for longer periods of time.

Punctuality should be observed in all business matters. Most business meetings begin with a handshake, regardless of the gender of those involved, especially if you are meeting for the first time. If the business relationship borders on a friendship, the greetings may be more demonstrative. Close associates may kiss each other on the cheek (if one is a woman) or they may embrace (if both are men).

Rushing straightforward into the topic of the meeting would be considered brash and rude. Business is conducted between two people, not between two firms, and as

For those who do not have a specific job but would like to work in Chile it is always risky to arrive in a country without any concrete leads. It is not impossible for a foreigner to find work in Chile in a corporation or non-governmental organization, but it will take a lot of dedication and a little luck. If you have any *pitutos* (connections) your search may prove more fruitful. Many Americans who set off to Chile in search of work end up as private English teachers and, although financially this line of work is viable, professionally it may not be the best alternative for you. If you cannot find a job, you will be unable to secure a visa to stay in Chile on a long-term basis and will have to exit every three months.

such a personal relationship needs to be developed. Chileans will always inquire about your family. This is not considered prying, but rather a friendly sign that they are truly interested. You should always ask about their families as well. If time is not a problem, it would be a good idea to briefly bring up other topics like Chilean wines, the salmon industry, the pension system or the economy in general before getting to the heart of the matter. It shows that you have taken the time to learn about Chile and also gives Chileans an opportunity to boast about how well their country is doing.

In keeping with the Chilean belief that plain is better and fancy is in bad taste, business cards should be kept very simple. Name, title, firm and contact information should be written in plain script. Do not attempt to dress it up with fancy colours, emblems or ornate logos.

Latin America is synonymous with graft for many people. This stereotype may have some basis in other countries, but in reality Chileans are generally honest. Grafting on all levels is considered a serious offense. In your business dealings with Chilean public officials you should be very careful not to imply that bribery is a bargaining tool.

Conducting Business in Chile

- Do arrive on time
- Do conduct business in an office
- Do dress conservatively
- Do take time to inquire about family (make it personal)
- Do not offer bribes

The Office Environment

Most likely you will experience some subtle differences between the Chilean workplace and the one to which you are accustomed. One major distinction is that the concept of "I'll get right on it!" does not exist in Chile. If you ask someone to do a specific task, do not expect them to drop what they are doing to attend to your request. Regardless of the importance of the matter, the Chilean will most likely say, "Yes, okay," which means "Just leave it with me and I'll get it done by the deadline." It will get done, but most things are done at the last minute, some only with prodding by nervous co-workers or bosses.

Chile ranks among the countries with the highest number of working hours per year. On average, Chileans work well over 2,000 hours a year, yet this does not necessarily translate into higher productivity.

One Chilean Undersecretary of Labour blamed it on the fact that Chileans tend to put things off, meaning they have to stay later at the office or go in on Saturdays. He also thought

Many Chileans are now employed in the fast growing service sector.

that Chileans do not work well in groups, or administer their time wisely. Of course, these are generalisations and, as in any culture, there are all types of workers. Moreover, it is important to remember that although Chileans are not as organised and productive as they potentially could be, the economy continues to do very well.

When Chileans work in groups on a specific project there is a tendency for one or two leaders to emerge. These leaders rise up to take responsibility and become much more involved in the project. As a result, they work much harder than the rest, who tend to lay back and let the others take control. Therefore, if questions or concerns arise, these members of the group appear to be 'passing the buck' instead of dealing with them head-on. It is important to determine which employees are actively involved in a specific project.

The ability to speak Spanish is a very important tool for anyone working in Chile. Most educated Chileans can read English and understand English, but not all are fluent. Thus, being able to speak and undrstand Spanish will not only impress your colleagues, but will help you to do your job well.

Guía Silber

The *Guía Silber* is a must for anyone wishing to do business in Chile. For those who are in Chile looking for work, it is the best place to begin. The *Guía Silber* is a comprehensive list providing the address and contact numbers of all government agencies, corporations, universities, non-governmental organisations, political parties, etc. However, it is not for sale in any bookstore. It must be purchased directly from the publisher, Silber Editores. It can be ordered online at their website (http://www.guiasilber. com). The phone number in Santiago is (02) 232-2400. The Publiguias Publishing House produces good business reference guides (including the *Yellow Pages* or *Paginas Amarillas*). The Internet is a growing source of valuable information. Overall, reference material in Chile is good and up to date.

Office Hours

Generally, office hours are from 8:30 am or 9:00 am to 5:30 pm or 6:00 pm from Monday to Friday, although many workers actually stay later. Banks are open Monday to Friday from 9:00 am to 2:00 pm. Government offices are open Monday to Friday, from 9:00 am to 6:00 pm, although some of them are open to the public only for limited periods during the day. Some offices may stay open even later depending on the workload. Chileans take a long lunch (one to two hours, although technically the lunch break should only be one hour). Most people in major urban areas do not go home or take a siesta.

In some countries employees will only do what is specifically outlined in their job description. In Chile, the atmosphere is much more relaxed and a Chilean employee will be more likely to take on any number of tasks when asked. Similarly, Chileans work late when required, are loyal to the company and expect loyalty in return.

Although many offices may appear to operate very informally, do not be deceived. There is a clear hierarchy within the office no matter how democratically it seems to function. As explained in the language chapter, the formal version of the word you (*usted*) is used in many situations. Furthermore, there are distinct class divisions among the office workers. Even though a secretary may be on very good terms with her boss, it is highly unlikely that they would associate outside of the office.

Attire

Office attire may be more formal in Chile than in your home country. Smart dressing is the norm. For the most part, there are no 'Dress down Fridays'. Short-sleeved dress shirts are acceptable in warm weather and sweater vests are often worn during the cold winter months. Men always wear a jacket and tie for business, with navy being the predominant colour. Men tend to put on their jackets when leaving the office, even just for lunch. Women dress conservatively, mainly in dresses, skirts or suits. Most secretaries and clerks in large firms such as banks and government agencies wear uniforms. This is particularly helpful to women from lower income families who do not have the money to spend on work clothes.

Employees

When hiring local workers in Chile, you may be surprised to find their high school listed on the curriculum vitae in addition to the university. Chileans have the habit of writing extremely long resumés overloaded with detailed information. However, naming the high school also serves a very important function. It indicates with whom the applicant studied and facilitates the use of the old-boy network.

A common practice is to specify gender, age or physical attributes in job advertisements. Most firms will ask for a photograph of the applicant for their file.

All offices employ a man known as a Junior. This person is responsible for miscellaneous errands. Juniors go to the bank, deliver documents (which makes courier services somewhat obsolete), purchase office supplies, etc. In many offices, the Junior also provides a number of personal services for other employees. However, this is not his job and is done only as a favour.

Each employee is responsible for paying for his or her personal long distance telephone calls, faxes, photocopies, etc. (Calls and faxes made regarding business are excluded.) At the end of the month, you might be expected to declare your personal calls and faxes. In some instances you are asked to keep track of personal photocopies on a nearby list. These amounts are then tallied and paid.

OTHER WORK MATTERS
Benefits

Employees are given 15 days paid vacation following the first year of employment. This amount increases with time. In addition, there are 12 public holidays in Chile. If the holiday falls on a weekend, the worker is not compensated with a weekday off, unless it is legally celebrated on the following Monday. When an employee is absent from work due to illness, a *licencia* (doctor's note) must be presented upon returning to the office. Health care and social security entitlements are discussed in detail below. In general, benefits are not negotiated during the hiring process, only salary and bonuses.

Health Care

In abidance with the law, a portion of every employee's salary (seven per cent) must be withheld for health care. The employee chooses the health care plan he or she wishes to join: the state system (FONASA) or one of the private plans called ISAPRES. Most salaried employees opt for an ISAPRE because the level of health care covered is substantially better than that provided by FONASA. There are a number of different ISAPRE plans from which the employee can choose. The plan is not tied to the place of employment.

Private Pension System

Chile implemented a reform of its pension fund system in the early 1980s. This successful programme has been studied by many other countries in the region, including the United States. All new workers entering the labour force must choose a private, for-profit Pension Fund Administrator (AFP). Workers who were already in the labour force at the time of the reform had the option of choosing a private company or staying with the old system.

Each employee has 10 per cent of his or her salary deducted. This money goes into his or her personal retirement account which is not tied to his or her place of work. A percentage of the deduction covers service charges, disability and survivor's benefits. Those wishing to surpass this limit or make a separate investment may make additional contributions to the AFP or open a separate

The AFP

The AFP is not without its critics. These criticisms include high administrative fees, low coverage (only about 55 per cent of the population have an AFP account), a 'loss of solidarity' (because the new system emphasises individual planning over large group funds), irregular practices to entice individuals to transfer to another AFP, loopholes that allow for early withdrawls, and cozy relations between the AFPs and the companies whose stock is being bought by the pension fund managers. In response to these allegations, a reform of the system is in the works.

savings account (linked to the performance of the fund) with either the same institution or a different one.

Workers choose their AFP according to level of risk and/or rate of return. Because the fund managers are private, there is ample opportunity for competition. AFPs have been tightly regulated by the government, but these restrictions are starting to loosen. AFPs can now invest abroad and in a wider array of domestic sectors. Currently, retirees receive higher pensions compared to the old system and workers know the exact amount of their retirement funds at all times. The government guarantees a minimum pension in the event that AFP payouts fall below the subsistence level. It has also dramatically raised savings in Chile, which now boasts the highest savings rate in Latin America, on par with developed countries.

Technically, foreign personnel under a work contract must have an AFP. Contributions are to be paid by both the company and the foreigner. However, if the foreign worker has social security outside Chile with basic provisions for illness, pension, disability, and death, then he or she may be exempt from making contributions. Check with your own country's Foreign Ministry to see if it has an agreement in place with Chile regarding pension benefits. Since retirement funds are kept in individual accounts handled by private pension funds that compete against each other, if you do join the Chilean system, it is important to do your homework and study the current and past performances of these funds.

Legalities

It is illegal to work in Chile while on a tourist or student visa. If you entered Chile on a tourist visa, you can apply at the Ministry of the Interior—*Extranjeria* (Foreigners Section) for a Work visa (*Sujeto a Contrato*). However, the proper procedure is to apply for the appropriate visa at a Chilean consulate prior to your arrival. The paperwork is substantial. You need a valid passport, a health certificate, a certificate from the police stating your good conduct and a notarised work contract from your firm, plus photos.

Freelance Work

It may appeal to you to do freelance work while in Chile, especially if your spouse has a work permit. Every time you receive payment for your work, you must give your client a receipt of honorarium or *Boleta de Honorarios*. You save a copy for your income tax declaration. You cannot be paid for work unless you provide your client with a *boleta*. Earnings are generally subject to a 10 per cent withholding tax, but you can negotiate with your clients whether your fee is *líquido* (net: the amount after the withholding tax) or *bruto* (gross: the full amount from which you yourself will pay the 10 per cent withholding). The income recorded on your *boletas* must be reported on your annual income tax declaration.

The paperwork is really overwhelming to get a *Boleta de Honorarios*, but well worth the effort. First, you must apply for an RUT (taxpayer identification number), which in and of itself requires major paperwork. Having been assigned an RUT you can then order the actual book of receipts, the *talonario de boletas*, at any small printer's shop. You must include your address, full name, field of activity and RUT. Every *boleta* in this book must be stamped by the *Servicio de Impuestos Internos*, the Chilean internal tax collector. In order to get that stamp, an application called *Iniciación de Actividades* must be completed. Do not be scared off though, the paperwork required in Chile is no more excessive than that required to work in other countries. Give yourself plenty of time to get the necessary papers and have it all approved.

The *Boleta de Honorarios* should not be confused with the sales receipt or *boleta*, which every merchant or service provider will give you for almost all transactions (as mandated by law). Unless you need them to justify expenses or to exchange an item, these *boletas*, which multiply like rabbits, are of no use.

When buying at large supermarkets, gas stations or stores selling intermediary goods you may be asked "*boleta o factura?*" meaning "sales receipt or invoice?" The *factura* or invoice is for individuals or corporations that can get VAT credit from the tax authorities. If you do not qualify, just answer *boleta* and pocket your newly acquired piece of paper.

Currency

The Chilean currency is the peso, which fluctuates between 500 and 550 to the US dollar. As in many other countries, periods distinguish thousands and commas denote fractions when writing numbers (for example, $ 5.000,30 is five thousand pesos and thirty cents). For simplicity, cents have been eliminated in accounting records.

The *Unidad de Fomento*, or UF, as it is commonly called, is a value unit that was created to account for inflation at a time when it had reached double-digit levels. The UF almost became a parallel currency. Most large ticket items that are paid over a long period of time, such as real estate, cars, rent, etc., are still priced in UFs or in the 'peso equivalent of the UF'. One UF is equal to a determined amount of pesos and this figure changes daily. Newspapers list the value of the UF in each issue. Also be careful to note that dates are written day/month/year.

Taxes

If a foreigner resides in Chile for six consecutive months within a calendar year or for more than a total of six months in two consecutive years, he or she is considered a resident and must pay taxes. Taxes for residents must be paid on income from either Chilean or foreign sources. Foreigners working in Chile, however, are only subject to taxes on their Chilean income during the first three years of residence, and this period may be extended. Beyond this extra period foreigners are subject to tax on their worldwide income. Taxes are annual, and are calculated on 31 December of each year. Tax returns must be filed in April each year on income earned in the preceding calendar year.

A real estate tax is levied on all property bought in Chile. The amount due is equal to two per cent of the fiscal valuation, and is payable in four installments (April, June, September and November).

Value Added Tax or IVA is 19 per cent in Chile and is already included in published prices (with the exception of capital goods and intermediary goods, where price is expressed as $ + IVA). By paying with US dollars, travellers cheques or a non-Chilean credit card a foreigner can avoid the hefty IVA charge at most hotels in Chile. Keep this in mind at check-out time.

Volunteer Work

For those who wish to do volunteer work in Chile, there are plenty of people and organisations that could use your help and volunteering is fairly easy. You can work with children, youth, women, the disabled or the aged. The best place to start is the website http://www.fundacionsoles.cl which provides a long list of charities and along with contact information, provides a short description of each. This foundation also publishes the *Guía Solidaria*, a good source for those who want to do something positive with their extra time.

FAST FACTS

CHAPTER 10

'It takes UFs to buy a DFL2.'
Chilean saying related to buying real estate.

Official Name
Republic of Chile

Flag
Two equal horizontal bands of white (top) and red; there is a blue square the same height as the white band at the hoist-side end of the white band; the square bears a white five-pointed star in the centre representing a guide to progress and honour. It is also a Mapuche symbol; blue symbolises the sky, white is for the snow-covered Andes and red stands for the blood spilled to achieve independence.

National Anthem
Himno Nacional de Chile.
To listen to the country's National Anthem and learn more about Chile's national symbols go to the government's website, http://www.chileangovernment.cl and look under National Symbols.

Time
Standard time zone: UTC/GMT -4 hours
Daylight saving time: + 1 hour

Country Code
56

Climate
Temperate; desert in north; Mediterranean in central region; cool and damp in south

Location
Southern South America, between the South Pacific Ocean and Argentina and bordering Peru and Bolivia to the north

Land Area
Total: 756,950 sq km (291,893 sq miles)
Land: 748,800 sq km (288.804 sq miles)
Water: 8,150 sq km (3,146.7 sq miles)

Natural Resources
Copper, timber, iron ore, nitrates, salt, zinc, precious metals, lithium, molybdenum, hydropower

Electricity
220 volts/50 Hz (plugs have two tubular pins)

Population
16,134,219 (July 2006 est.)

Ethnic Groups
White and white-Amerindian 95 per cent, Amerindian 3 per cent, other 2 per cent

Religion
Roman Catholic 70 per cent, Protestant 15 per cent, other faiths, 6 per cent and agnostic 8 per cent (other faiths includes, Jehovas Witnesses, Mormons, Jews, Muslims, Orthodox and others)

Official Language
Spanish

Government
Unitarian Republic

Capital
Santiago

Administrative Divisions
Chile is made up of 14 regions and the Metropolitan Region of Santiago. A recent reform increased the number of regions from 12 to 14. Previously, regions were known by their number more than their name. In order from north to south: Arica y Parinacota (13th, new); Tarapacá (1st); Antofagasta (2nd); Atacama (3rd); Coquimbo (4th); Valparaíso (5th); Libertador General Bernardo O'Higgins (6th); Maule (7th); Bío Bío (8th); Araucanía (9th); Valdivia (14th, new); Los Lagos (10th); Aysén del General Carlos Ibáñez del Campo (11th); Magallanes y la Antártica Chilena (12th); Región Metropolitana (Santiago)

Currency
Chilean peso (CLP)

Gross Domestic Product (GDP)
US$ 118.2 billion (2006)

Agriculture Products
Grapes, apples, pears, onions, tomatoes, wheat, corn, oats, peaches, plums, kiwi, garlic, asparagus, beans, beef, poultry, wool, fish and timber.

Industries
Copper, other minerals, foodstuffs, fish processing, iron and steel, wood and wood products, transport equipment, cement and textiles.

Exports
Copper, fruit, fishmeal and fish, paper and pulp, chemicals and wine.

Imports

Petroleum and petroleum products, chemicals, electrical and telecommunications equipment, heavy industrial machinery, vehicles, natural gas, consumer products and food

Taxes

19 per cent value added tax (IVA)

Airport Tax for International Flights

US$ 18
Airport tax for domestic flights is included in ticket price

Life Expectancy

76.7 years

Literacy Rate/Education

95.8 per cent are literate
98.6 per cent attend primary school
92.6 per cent attend secondary school
37.5 per cent have higher education

Viñedos propiedad
Viña Concha y Toro

Chile is a major exporter of wines. Most vineyards are located in the Central Valley.

Quality of Life Indicators

96 per cent of homes have access to electricity

91 per cent of homes have access to drinkable water

52 per cent of homes have a telephone

21 per cent of homes have a computer

10 per cent of homes have access to the Internet

NOTABLE NAMES

Pedro de Valdivia (early 1500s)

Conquistador and founder of the cities of Santiago, Concepción and Valdivia.

Bernardo O´Higgins (1778-1842)

Liberator of Chile from Spanish rule and first head of state.

Arturo Prat (1848-1879)

One of Chile's greatest heroes. As Captain of the *Esmeralda* naval ship during the Battle of Iquique, he showed great bravery when he jumped aboard the enemy ship and was subsequently killed.

Salvador Allende

First socialist elected President of Chile. He died in the 11 September 1973 Coup led by General Augusto Pinochet.

General Augusto Pinochet

Military general who took power in the 1973 coup and ruled until 1989.

Michelle Bachelet

First female President of Chile, she took office in 2006.

Sebastián Piñera

Entrepreneur and Congressman who is one of the leaders of the Chilean right.

Joaquín Lavín

Former mayor of Santiago and Presidential Candidate, he is another important figure in the Chilean political right.

Soledad Alvear
Senator and former Minister, she is also leader of the Christian Democratic Party.

Pablo Neruda
Poet who won the Nobel Prize for Literature in 1971

Gabriela Mistral
Poet who won the Nobel Prize in Literature in 1945.

Isabel Allende
Popular author of several novels and memoirs.

José Donoso
Well-known author and member of the Latin American Boom.

Padre Alberto Hurtado
Priest who took care of homeless children and founded the Hogar de Cristo foundation. He died in 1952 and was made a Saint in 2005.

Cecilia Bolocco
She was crowned Miss Universe in 1987.

Marcelo Ríos
Top-seeded tennis player. He was the first Latin American player to reach the number one position.

Nicolás Massú
Tennis player. He won two gold medals at the Athens Summer Olympics in 2004.

Don Francisco
Host of the popular *Sabado Gigante* televisión programme seen throughout Latin America.

Roberto Matta (1911-2002)
Famous surrealist painter.

Claudio Arrau (1903-1991)
Highly respected classical pianist.

Eliseo Salazar
Retired, international race car driver who has competed in the Gran Prix of Monaco, Le Mans and the Indianapolis 500.

PLACES OF INTEREST

- Lago Chungará—beautiful emerald lake up in the Altiplano surrounded by volcanoes.
- Town of La Tirana—go for the colourful La Tirana festival in July.
- San Pedro de Atacama—picturesque town famous for its colonial church and archeological museum.
- Valle de la Luna—valley that due to its mineral composition and wind erosion gives the traveller the impression of being on the moon. Near San Pedro de Atacama.
- Tatio Geysers—geysers that erupt at sunrise daily
- La Serena—beautiful city with long beaches. Visit the nearby Valle del Elqui and the Gabriela Mistral Museum in Vicuña.
- Zapallar/Cachagua beaches—take your binoculars to see the penguin colony on the island off of the beach at Cachagua
- Viña del Mar—Seaside resort with restaurants, beaches, shopping and a casino.
- Valparaíso—interesting city noted for the Pablo Neruda house, funicular rides up the hills and port
- Isla Negra—Pablo Neruda house with his collections of ship's mastheads and coloured glass
- Viña Concha y Toro—vineyard near Santiago with tours, wine shop and wine tasting
- Viña Santa Rita—beautiful setting amid the mountains, vineyard offers tours, wine tasting and a nice restaurant
- Cajón del Maipo—canyon just southeast of Santiago that is perfect for daytrips. Various activities include swimming, hiking and horseback riding. There are many restaurants and simple hotels if you want to spend the night.
- Pomaire—small town near Santiago known for its pottery.

The Museo Histórico Nacional (National History Museum) occupies the former Real Audiencia (colonial tribunal) on the Plaza de Armas.

- La Campana National Park—park with the last existing Chilean Palm tree forest. The Campana hill can also be climbed.
- Pucón—town at the foot of the Villarrica volcano, a centre for many outdoor activities
- Valdivia—tour the 17th century Spanish forts at Corral, Niebla and Isla Mancera.
- Termas de Puyehue—grand hotel with hot springs, outdoor activities and spectacular views.
- Puerto Varas and Frutillar—two small towns on Lago Llanquihue facing the Osorno Volcano. Frutillar is home to the German Museum and hosts the annual classical music festival. From Puerto Varas you can easily access the Saltos de Petrohué, the Lago Todos los Santos and the city of Puerto Montt.
- Chiloé—this island is known for its houses on stilts (*palafitos*) and brightly painted wooden churches.
- Laguna San Rafael—home to the San Valentín glacier. You can get up close and drink whisky poured over small pieces of the glacier found floating in the lake.
- Torres del Paine National Park—beautiful park known for the Cuernos del Paine (Horns of Paine). Park is home to glaciers, lakes and hiking trails. Activities include camping, hiking, climbing, kayaking and glacier crossing.
- Easter Island—Noted for its mysterious Moai stone sculptures and Polynesian history and culture.

ACRONYMS

AFP	A privately administered pension fund
CODELCO	National Chilean Copper Company
FACH	Air Force of Chile
FFAA	Fuerzas Armadas (Armed Forces)
FONASA	Public health care system
IVA	Impuesto al Valor Agregado (Value Added Tax—VAT)
La U	Short form for the University of Chile
MERCOSUR	Southern Cone Common Market
ONG	Organización No Gubernental (NGO)
PC	Partido Comunista (Communist Party)

PDC	Partido Demócrata Cristiano (Christian Democratic Party)
PPD	Partido por la Democracia (Party for Democracy)
PS	Partido Socialista (Socialist Party)
RN	Renovación Nacional (National Renewal Party)
RUN	Rol Unico Nacional (Civil registry ID number)
RUT	Tax Identification Number
SA	Sociedad Anónima (part of a publicly traded corporation's name)
SERNATUR	Servicio Nacional de Turismo (National Tourism Service)
UC	Universidad Católica (Catholic University)
UDI	Unión Demócrata Independiente (National Democratic Union Party)
UE	Unión Europea (European Union)
UF	Unidad de Fomento (monetary value index)
q. (in handwriting)	que (that, which)

CULTURE QUIZ

SITUATION ONE

You are a businessperson who studied in Chile. You have an appointment with a local Chilean firm and you are delighted to encounter an old school friend who is now a manager at the firm. Your appointment is actually with your friend's superior, who is a good deal older than you. Later, your friend invites you home to meet his spouse, children and parents, who all live together. At dinner, you are served by the maid, who is an excellent cook, and you compliment her cooking abilities. Should you use *tú* or *Usted* with the a) friend b) superior c) spouse d) children e) parents f) maid?

Comments

Your friend should be addressed as *tú*, as you probably began the relationship on that basis when you were students, and you are approximately the same age.

Since you have never met your friend's superior before, *Usted* would be used. The superior is also in a high position, is older, and the pretext for the conversation is business, all reasons to use *Usted*.

The spouse should be addressed as *tú*. Even though you have not met before, the spouse is married to your friend. The children should be addressed as *tú*, as they are a great deal younger than you.

The parents of your friend would be addressed as *Usted*. You have never met them before and they are older. Even if you were the same approximate age as the parents, it would be best to use *Usted* because your connection to them is through their child.

The maid should be addressed as *Usted*. Anyone in service positions should be treated with the respect that *Usted* implies.

Remember that the children will probably use *Usted* with you, and the parents will probably use *tú*, even though you will use the opposite with them. This does not mean that you should change the form used. Only the parents, perhaps, after a time, will invite you to *tutear*, effectively acknowledging that you are equals. The invitation can only be extended by the superior, and should not be extended to children or hired help.

SITUATION TWO

You are invited to a party at a Chilean's house. There are around 20 people there when you arrive. You only know five of these people, including the host. As you first enter the room you:

A Go immediately to the people you know, avoiding eye contact with the strangers, simply saying "Hello" to your friends.

B Greet the host, then work your way around the room slowly, kissing the right cheek of every person if you are female, or, if you are male, shaking hands with other males and kissing the cheek of the females.

C Go up to the host, thank him or her for inviting you, and expect the host to introduce you to the others.

Comments

If you were to act as in **Ⓐ**, Chileans would think you very rude. Latinos make a lot of eye contact, so much so it seems at times like long-distance flirting or at least a good sizing-up. If you limit your contact to those whom you already know, it may insult the host, as he or she invited all the people whom they thought would get along well together. Of course, there will be some clustering among intimate friends, but at a large party one is expected to mingle. A verbal greeting is not sufficient in a social setting in Chile, cheek-kissing and shaking hands is the norm.

Ⓑ is the correct choice. The host should be greeted first, but try and keep it brief to avoid monopolising the host and losing your window of opportunity to introduce yourself. Chileans are not shy at parties, and they have no reservations about going up to complete strangers and introducing themselves. If you find someone really interesting to talk to while on this preliminary survey of the party, resist the temptation to stop and chat. Instead quickly finish introducing yourself to everyone and then return.

Chileans for the most part do not need a third party to introduce themselves to strangers in a social setting, as in **Ⓒ**. Perhaps if you are a VIP, or speak no Spanish, the host will introduce you, but for the most part you are on your own.

SITUATION THREE

You run a red light and as a result have a minor car accident in Santiago. The *Carabineros* come and take your license. You should:

Ⓐ Say repeatedly that you are a foreigner and they have no right to take away your license.

Ⓑ Quietly take the *Carabinero* aside and offer him some pesos.

Ⓒ Take the ticket and drive without your license until your court date.

Comments

Ⓐ is an all too common response. However, the police in Chile do have the right to take your license if you have committed a minor violation. Just because the Chilean laws are not how you think they should be does not make you exempt from these laws. Some foreigners think that their passports give them unique legal status, but this is not the case.

❸ would work well in many Latin American countries, but not in Chile. It could get you into big trouble, so don't risk it.

❸ is the right answer. If you have any questions on the correct procedure to get your license back you can call the offices of the municipality where the incident occurred.

SITUATION FOUR

After working for a few weeks in a Chilean office you go out for drinks with your co-workers. It comes out in the course of discussion that the majority of these Chileans are pro-Pinochet. You can:

❹ Get into a heated debate, citing the terrible human rights abuses committed under his regime.

❸ Listen to what they have to say and try and be non-judgmental.

❸ Ask who won the latest soccer game and change the subject.

Comments

❹ is most foreigners' gut response, but not a good choice given that around 40 per cent of Chileans supported Pinochet when he stepped down, and many still admire the man. It may be hard for you to imagine what would allow Chileans to continue to hold Pinochet in high esteem. A heated debate may feel like the right thing to do at the moment, but it will not change anyone's opinion. Plus it may make your life at work a bit uncomfortable.

❸ is an option if your blood pressure can handle it. It is interesting to hear the other side in debates that seem to foreigners so obviously one-sided. It will provide you with insight into the political beliefs of a significant portion of the population. Laura once listened intently to a conversation giving all the benefits of Amazon deforestation. It did not change her opinion, but it was a learning experience.

If you are unable to keep calm for ❸, and want to stay out of trouble, then ❸ is the best exit out of a thorny situation.

SITUATION FIVE

A close Chilean friend whom you haven't seen in several months invites you over for *once*. Upon arrival, as she kisses you on the cheek, your friend exclaims, "My God, how you have gained weight! You look so fat!" You can:

❹ Grimace, force back the tears, and tell your friend that you are considering liposuction.

❸ Glare and decide to never call this person again.

❸ Smile and remark on your friend's appearance.

Comments

❹ is a normal response to what seems like a very cutting comment. Chilean honesty in matters of appearance takes some getting accustomed to.

❸ would be a mistake, as this Chilean is not a bad person, just someone who has been raised in Chilean society, where comments that you consider to be cruel are not meant to be so. Giving a false opinion of someone's appearance would, for a Chilean, be viewed as unnecessary. So take this remark as a sign of intimacy with your friend.

❸ is the best response, once you are able to go against your first instinct of being insulted.

SITUATION SIX

You become friendly with the landlady who owns your apartment. She obviously has some Mapuche or other Amerindian blood from her skin tone and features. You start talking about your upcoming trip to the Lake District. When you ask if anyone in her family still speaks Mapuche, the landlady becomes visibly offended, mutters an excuse, and leaves quickly. What happened?

❹ The landlady hates the Mapuche.

❸ The landlady is offended by a personal question.

❸ The landlady is insulted that you consider her to be part Mapuche.

Comments

Ⓐ is very unlikely. Most Chileans respect the Mapuche and consider them to be an important part of Chile, although disconnected from mainstream Chilean culture.

Ⓑ is also unlikely, as Chileans have no problems answering questions about their family history and actually welcome your interest.

Ⓒ is most likely the case. Although there was much mixing between the Amerindians and the Spanish in the early days of colonization, Chileans identify themselves as mainly of European descent because the dominant culture and language is European based. A much better question to pose to a Chilean is from which part of the world their ancestors came.

SITUATION SEVEN

You are a businessperson who lives and works in Chile. You would like to do something nice for a Chilean business associate. You:

Ⓐ Invite the Chilean for a round of golf at your club.

Ⓑ Take the Chilean out to the nightclubs for a night of drinking.

Ⓒ Invite the Chilean to your home for dinner.

Comments

Ⓐ While business smooching over a round of golf is common in many countries, Chile has not been caught up in the golfing craze. Chilean businesspeople are generally not avid golfers and it would be uncomfortable for someone to have to turn down your invitation because they don't know how to play. However, inviting the Chileans who are already members of your golf club to a round would be a perfect way to establish friendships.

Ⓑ Again, a night of free drinks is de riguer in many lands to cement a business relationship, but not particularly so in Chile. Some Chileans may take you up on your offer, but this behaviour is not expected. In addition, it may not be the exact image you want to project. Others will politely refuse your invitation. If you insist, you may come off as annoying.

The best choice is **C** A quiet dinner in your home is the perfect way to socialise with any Chilean, and it is an important part of doing business in Chile. While the reputation of your company obviously matters, Chileans like to think that they are doing business with individuals, not just nameless representatives. It is much better to establish these close friendships as the Chileans do, in their homes. Of course, while Chilean businesspeople do occasionally take clients out to a restaurant, it is preferable to eventually introduce your business associates to your family in your home.

SITUATION EIGHT

You make friends with a single expatriate woman. While in Chile she meets a Chilean man and they begin a romantic relationship. You accompany the new couple to dinner and a show, and in the course of the evening you discover that the man is in his mid-30s yet lives at home with his parents, never worked until finishing his advanced degree and insists on seeing your woman friend every day. The next day your friend asks your opinion of her new boyfriend. What do you think?

A Obviously a wierdo. You tell your friend to run as fast as she can.

B Seems like a typical Chilean. You wish her happiness in the relationship.

Comments

While **A** may be many foreigners' initial impression, all of the above behaviours are typical in Chile and in no way indicate deviant conduct.

B is the appropriate response. It may be hard to believe that the man is not a total loser, but he is only behaving as Chilean society would have good sons and male suitors conduct themselves. In many cultures, a man this age who lives at home would be considered strange. But in Chile a single man who has just entered the job market often stays on at home for the convenience of free food, laundry and cleaning. He feels no pressure to leave either from his family or society. Another important factor is the intensity of family bonds in Chile, where even married children may choose to live with their parents. The possessiveness of *pololeando*, or dating, in Chile may appear extreme, but is considered normal in their culture. His desire to see her and talk to her constantly is a typical expression of his fondness for her.

SITUATION NINE

You are just arriving in Chile for a temporary, but long stay. You are in the process of settling in and buying the many things you will need. You decide that you need to buy **Ⓐ** a car; **Ⓑ** some furniture; **Ⓒ** some food for the refrigerator; and **Ⓓ** some Chilean knick-knacks to make the house look homey. Are the prices for these items set in stone or do you bargain to get a better price?

Comments

Ⓐ Car. Negotiate the price. You can expect to get about a 10 per cent discount off the sticker price.

Ⓑ Furniture. Depends. If you are looking to buy furniture in a department store expect to pay the amount on the price tag. At furniture stores, if you pay cash or buy multiple items, you can ask for a discount.

Ⓒ Food. Set price. Whether you are buying food at a super-market, at an open air market (*feria*), or even from a guy selling a bag of avocados on the corner, you pay the price asked.

Ⓓ Knick-knacks. Depends. If you are buying knick-knacks in a store you need to pay the asking price. Even at a *feria* in the city, vendors may be unwilling to haggle. However, if you are in a rural area or are buying large quantities, you might be able to negotiate a better price.

DO'S AND DON'TS

DO'S

- Greet those you know or are introduced to with a kiss on the cheek for women or with a handshake between men if it is a casual setting. In business meetings, shake hands regardless of the person's gender.
- Go out of your way to greet someone you run into. (Waving, then walking on is not enough.)
- Make it a point to ask your Chilean friends and colleagues about their families.
- Bring a gift, such as flowers or chocolate, for your hostess when invited to dinner.
- Invite your Chilean friends home for dinner at least once (this is preferable to taking them out to a restaurant or bar).
- Arrive about 15 minutes late for a social event.
- Expect to eat dinner late, usually not before 9:00 pm.
- Dress well, even to informal events. Jeans should really be worn only to an *asado* (picnic).
- Try to use any Spanish you have learned; it will be greatly appreciated.
- Remove your hat when indoors.
- Say you must be going about 10 minutes before you actually get up to leave.
- Escort a woman all the way home after an evening out (if you are a man), even if you are merely friends.
- Pay for dinner for anyone you've invited out to dinner, no matter how informally.
- Arrive on time for a business meeting.
- Conduct business in a formal setting, i.e., at the office.
- Use *Usted* (the formal 'you') with business associates and those you have just met.
- Get a *licencia* (doctor's note) if you miss work due to illness.
- Tip just about everyone who serves you: 10 per cent for waiters; some small change for gas station attendants, grocery store baggers and *cuidadores de autos* (people who watch your parked car).

- Give the mailman a little money at the end of the month. Technically you owe a couple of pesos for each piece of mail delivered.
- Protect against pollution, especially in winter, by avoiding strenuous outdoor activities.
- Cover your mouth when yawning.

DON'TS
- Rush straight into business negotiations. Start by chatting.
- Dress or behave in a flamboyant fashion. Err on the conservative side, right down to your business card.
- Chew gum in any formal or semi-formal situation.
- Remove your shoes when entering a home.
- Smoke at someone's house without asking for permission.
- Be insulted if anyone calls you 'gringo;' it is used as a term of endearment.
- Be insulted by blunt comments on your appearance.
- Ask others how much their personal items (e.g. jewellery or watches) cost.
- Assume that all Chileans are anti-Pinochet.
- Leave your host's home immediately after the meal. Expect to stay at least an hour longer.
- Bounce a check; it is illegal and you could face severe penalties.
- Offer bribes.
- Drive your car if you have *Restricción* due to a pollution emergency.

GLOSSARY

PUBLIC RESTROOMS

Spanish	English
baños	bathrooms
hombres/caballeros	men
mujeres/damas	women
occupado/a	occupied
libre	vacant, unoccupied
C/F (on faucet)	*caliente* (hot)/*frío* (cold)

PUBLIC BUILDINGS

Spanish	English
no fumar/prohibido fumar	no smoking/smoking is forbidden
entrada	entrance
salida	exit

ON DOORS

Spanish	English
empuje	push
tire	pull

SHOPPING

Spanish	English
horario de atención	working hours
cerrado/a	closed
fuera de servicio	out of order
privado	private
informaciones	information
gratis	free of charge
caja	cashier/payment desk

Spanish	English
empaque	where your purchase is wrapped and handed to you
liquidación	sale

RESTAURANTS

Spanish	English
Que desean? *Que van a servirse?*	What would you like to order?
La cuenta por favor	The check, please.
Con o sin hielo?	Would you like your drink with or without ice?
Natural or helado	Would you like your beverage room temperature or chilled?
Con o sin espuma?	Would you like your beer with or without a head?
Apunto/término medio/ bien cocida	rare/medium rare/ well done (meat)
Colación	set lunch with fixed price (normally cheaper than ordering separately)

TRAVELLING

Spanish	English
aeropuerto	airport
terminal de buses	bus station
estación de trenes	train station
ida/ida y vuelta	single/round trip
primera/segunda clase	first/second class
micro	city bus
liebre	small bus

Spanish	English
colectivo	collective taxi running a specific route
boleto	bus, plane or train ticket
parte/multa	ticket for traffic violation
Restricción	a system preventing drivers from driving during pollution emergencies based on the last number on the car's license plate
minusválido	physically handicapped person
pare	stop
reduzca velocidad	slow down
lento	slow
ceda el paso	yield
calle de un solo sentido	one-way street
en rodaje	slow vehicle
radiopatrulla	police cruiser

AT THE CORREO (POST OFFICE)

Spanish	English
carta	letter
estampillas/sellos	stamps
tarjeta postal	postcard
correo aéreo	airmail
encomienda	parcel to be mailed

DANGER

Spanish	English
cuidado	caution
peligro	danger

Spanish	English
alta tensión	high voltage
socorro!	help!
prohibido nadar	no swimming allowed
bomberos	firemen
Carabineros	police (uniformed)

HOME & SCHOOL

Spanish	English
se vende/se arrienda	for sale/rent
gastos comunes	condominium fees
empleada 'puertas afuera'	maid who works normal working hours
empleada 'puertas adentro'	live-in maid
maestro 'chasquilla'	handyman, idiom for Jack of All Trades
gásfiter	plumber
electricista	electrician
jardín infantíl	nursery school
escuela	grammar school
liceo or colegio	high school
particular/público	private/public
particular subvencionado	publicly funded, privately administered

RESOURCE GUIDE

EMERGENCY AND HEALTH
Emergency Numbers
- Uniformed police (*Carabineros*) 133
- Detectives (*Investigaciones*) 134
- Ambulance (*Ambulancias*) 131
- Fire (*Bomberos*) 132
- Poisoning 635-3800 (dial 02 before the number if calling from points outside of Santiago)

TRANSPORT & COMMUNICATIONS
Telephone
- Country Code 56

City Codes:
- Antofagasta 55
- Chillán 42
- Iquique 57
- Puerto Montt 65
- Rancagua 72
- Talca 71
- Valdivia 63
- Arica 58
- Concepción 41
- La Serena 51
- Punta Arenas 61
- Santiago 02
- Temuco 45
- Valparaíso/Viña del Mar 32

Postal Service
The main post office in Santiago is Correo Central, Plaza de Armas de Santiago 983. Tel: (02) 697-1701

Internet Service Providers
- ENTEL Internet
  Website: http://www.entelchile.net
- CTC Internet
  Website: http://www.telefonicachile.cl
- VTR Internet
  Website: http://www.vtr.cl
- Manquehue
  Website: http://www.manquehue.net

Embassies

- Australian Embassy
  Isidora Goyenechea 3621, 13th Fl. Las Condes,
  Santiago. Tel: (02) 550-3500
  Website: http://www.chile.embassy.gov.au
- British Embassy
  Avenida El Bosque Norte 0125, Santiago.
  Tel: (02) 370-4100
  Website: http://www.britemb.cl
- Canadian Embassy
  Nueva Tajamar 481 #12 Torre Norte
  (World Trade Center Building), Santiago.
  Tel: (02) 652-3800
- Embassy of the United States of America
  Avenida Andrés Bello 2800, Santiago. Tel: (02) 232-2600
  Website: http://www.usembassy.cl
- French Embassy
  Avenida Condell 65, Santiago. Tel: (02) 470-8000
- German Embassy
  Las Hualtatas 5677, Vitacura. Tel: (02) 463-2500
  Website: http://www.santiago.diplo.de

HOSPITALS AND DENTAL CLINICS

These clinics in Santiago should have English-speaking
doctors and dentists. For further references, contact the US
or British Embassy.

- Clínica Alemana
  Avenida Vitacura 5951. Tel: (02) 210-1111
  Website: http://www.alemana.cl
- Centro Médico Clínica Alemana de La Dehesa
  Avenida José Alcalde Delano 12205.
  Tel: (02) 586-1700, 586-1753 (emergency)
- Clínica Las Condes
  Lo Fontecilla 441.
  Tel: (02) 210-4000, 210-5150 (emergency)
  Website: http://www.clc.cl
- Clínica Reñaca
  Anabaena 336—Reñaca, Viña del Mar.
  Tel: (032) 265-8000

- Clínica Santa María
  Avenida Santa María 0500, Providencia.
  Tel: (02) 461-2000. Website: http://www.csm.cl
- Clínica Vitacura
  Avenida Presidente Kennedy 3210, Vitacura.
  Tel: (02) 477-5600
  Website: http://www.clinicavitacura.cl
- Centro Médico
  Avenida Vitacura 3197. Tel: (02) 477-5640
- Centro Odontológico Padre Mariano
  Alcántara 295, Las Condes. Tel: (02) 485-7000
  Website: http://www.padremariano.com
- Clínica Dental Estoril
  Paul Harris 10349, Las Condes. Tel: (02) 215-1021

SPORTS & FITNESS CENTRES (GIMNASIOS)

- Fisic. Avenida Tobalaba 607, Santiago. Tel: (02) 232-6641
- Club Pato Cornejo. Monseñor Escrivá de Balaguer,
  Lo Barnechea 12352. Tel: (02) 217-2031
  Website: http://www.clubpatocornejo.cl
- Sportlife. Camino el Alba 11865, Las Condes
  Tel: (02) 214-2257 or 214-5188
  Website: http://www.sportlife.cl
- Gimnasio Sésamo. Avenida Los Leones 2384,
  Providencia. Tel: (02) 204-2770
  Website: http://www.sesamo.cl
- YMCA. Compañía 1360, Santiago. Tel: (02) 696-5106
- Club Deportivo de la Universidad Católica Santa Rosa de
  las Condes. Avenida Andrés Bello 2782, Las Condes.
  Tel: (02) 412-4400. Website: http://www2.lacatolica.cl
- Spaclub Providencia. Avenida Jorge Matte Gormaz 1650.
  Tel: (02) 225-0465 or 223-2773

FACILITIES FOR THE DISABLED

In general, Chile is not a disabled-friendly country, although
progress is being made. In the downtown area and in new
neighbourhoods, sidewalks are wheelchair friendly. Some
subway stations in Santiago have escalators and elevators.
Ramps are rare, but newer buildings will have them as well

as special elevators and toilets for the disabled. For more details, contact:

- Asociación Chilena de Lisiados (Chilean Association of Handicapped Persons) Lira 134, Santiago.
  Tel: (02) 639-0226

HOME & FAMILY
Relocation & Accommodation

See *Welcome to Chile*, a guide published by the Chilean-American Chamber of Commerce, and the *Propiedades* section of the *El Mercurio* newspaper (www.propiedades. elmercurio.com). Real estate agents are widely used for buying and renting property and relocation companies can help with all the details. Among the best known:

- Gamio Real Estate and Relocation
  Presidente Errazuriz 3376, Las Condes. Tel: (02) 233-8200
  Website: http://www.gamiopropiedades.com
  (English speaking)
- Contact Chile
  Huelén 219, Providencia. Tel: (02) 264-1719
  Website: http:// www.contactchile.cl
  (English and German speaking)
- ACOP. Avenida Providencia 2008-A, Santiago.
  Tel: (02) 366-0414. Website: http://www.acop.cl
- Pro Casa. Las Hortensias 2994, Santiago;
  Tel: (02) 231-1971. Website: http://www.procasa.cl
- Portal Inmobiliario is a web portal for dozens of real estate companies. http://www.portalinmobiliario.cl
- OLAM/ CAI Relocation Services (Chilean branch of Cultural Awareness International, USA)
  2626 Cole Ave., Suite 710, Dallas, TX 75204. USA.
  Tel: (214) 691-4113 (USA). Tel: (02) 475-0758 (Chile)

CHILDCARE & EDUCATION

- *Ministerio de Educación* (Ministry of Education)
  Website: http://www.mineduc.cl.

Other useful websites

- http://www.buscacolegio.cl.
- http://www.english-schools.org/chile

Free/subsidised municipal schools, please check with the *Corporación de Educación* of your *Comuna* (municipality). For private schools and kindergartens/nurseries, check the *Yellow Pages* (http://www.amarillas.cl) under *Colegios* and *Jardines Infantiles* respectively. For universities check out http://www.ues.cl

English Schools

- Colegio Nido de Aguilas (The American School)
  Avenida El Rodeo 4200, Lo Barnechea.
  Tel: (02) 339-8100. Website: http://www.nido.cl
- The Grange School (British)
  Avenida Príncipe de Gales 6154, La Reina.
  Tel: (02) 586-0100. Website: http://www.grange.cl
- Santiago College (British)
  Lota 2465, Providencia. Tel: (02) 751-3800
  Website: http://www.scollege.cl
- Redland School (British)
  Camino Las Flores 10121 (elementary school)
  Camino El Alba 11357 (middle and upper school)
  Las Condes Tel: (02) 959-8500
- Lincoln International Academy (English)
  Avenida Las Condes 13150. Tel: (02) 496-7600
  Website: http://www.lintac.cl
- St. Gabriel's School (British)
  Avenida Bilboa con Tobalaba. Tel: (02) 462-5400
  Website: http://www.saintgabriels.cl
- St. George´s College (British)
  Avenida Américo Vespucio Norte 5400, Vitacura.
  Tel: (02) 355-6100
  Website: http://www.saintgeorge.cl
- Craighouse (British)
  Avenida El Rodeo 12525, Lo Barnechea.
  Tel: (02) 756-0200. Website: http://www.craighouse.cl
- The Mayflower School (British)
  Avenida Las Condes 12167, Las Condes.
  Tel: (02) 217-1085

French School

- Lycèe A. De Saint-Exupéry (Alianza Francesa)
  Avenida Luis Pasteur 5418, Santiago. Tel: (02) 218-5151
  Website: http://www.lafase.cl

German Schools

- Deutsche Schule Colegio Alemán de Santiago (German)
  Nuestra Señora del Rosario 850.
  Tel: (02) 424-6100 (elementary school)
  Avenida Kennedy 6150.
  Tel: (02) 212-8499 (middle and high school).
  Website: http://www.dsstgo.cl
- Colegio Suizo (German)
  José Domingo Cañas 2206, Ñuñoa.
  Tel: (02) 379-2727. Website: http://www.css.cl

Hebrew School

- Instituto Hebreo Dr. Chaim Weizmann
  Avenida Las Condes 13450, Lo Barnechea.
  Tel: (02) 941-7900. Website: http://www.institutohebreo.cl

Italian School

- Scuola Italiana (Italian)
  Avenida Apoquindo 4836, Santiago.
  Tel: (02) 206-1920. Website: http://www.scuola.cl

Language Institutes

- Centro Chileno-Canadiense
  Avenida Luis Thayer Ojeda Norte 0191 Of. 601,
  Providencia. Tel: (02) 334-1090
  Website: http://www.canadiense.cl
- Berlitz
  Website: http://www.berlitz.cl
- Instituto Chileno Norteamericano
  Moneda 1467, Santiago. Tel: (02) 696-3215
  Website: http://www.norteamericano.cl
- The English Connection
  Bucarest 207 # 3, Providencia. Tel: (02) 335-3033
  Website: http://www.englishconnection.cl

- Goethe Institut
  Esmeralda 650, Santiago. Tel: (02) 462-1800
  Website: http://www.goethe.de/santiago/

Housekeeping Services

Full- and part-time housekeepers are common. Word of mouth is the most common way to find an *empleada/asesora* (maid) or *nana* (nanny). Check the *Empleo-Personal para el Hogar* (Employment-Housekeeping) section of the *El Mercurio* newspaper and *Agencias de Empleo* (job agencies).

MANAGING YOUR MONEY

One of the best sources on banking and financial matters is the website: http://www.amchamchile.cl, the official website of the American Chamber of Commerce. See also Doing Business and Investing in Chile by PriceWaterhouse Coopers at http://www.pwcglobal.com

Banks and Financial Services

- Banco de Chile. Website: http://www.bancochile.cl
  (check website for branch locations)
- Banco SantanderSantiago
  Website: http://www.santandersantiago.cl
- Citibank. Website: http://www.citibank.cl
- Chilena Consolidada Seguros (Insurance)
  Avenida Pedro de Valdivia 195, Providencia.
  Tel: (600) 600-9090 or (02) 200-7000
  Website: http://www.chilena.cl
- Consorcio (Financial Services)
  Avenida El Bosque 180, Santiago.
  Tel: (600) 221-3000 or (02) 782 5398
  Website: http://www.consorcio.cl

HOTEL
Luxury Hotels

- Grand Hyatt Santiago
  Avenida Kennedy 4601. Tel: (02) 950-1231
  Website: http://www.santiago.grandhyatt.com

- Marriott Santiago.
  Avenida Kennedy 5741. Tel: (02) 426-2000.
  Website: http://www.marriott.com
- Sheraton Hotel and Towers
  Avenida Santa Maria 1742. Tel: (02) 233-5000
  Website: http://www.sheraton.com/santiago/

Apart Hotels
- http://www.chilestay.com
- http://www.chile-hotels.com
- http://www.contactchile.cl
- http://www.chilecontact.com
- http://www.santiago.biz-stay.com
- http://www.santamagdalena.cl
- http://www.topapart.cl
- http://www.rentahome.cl
- http://www.apartelbosque.cl

CINEMAS & THEATRES
Most movies are screened in the original language (usually English) with Spanish subtitles, but children's movies are dubbed. Besides revamped old movie houses, US-style multiplexes are popping up in every mall. Theatre is almost exclusively Spanish. Check the papers or the Website: http://www.laguiadesantiago.cl for listings.

- Cinemark Alto Las Condes. Tel: (600) 600-2463
- Showcase Cinemas Parque Arauco. Tel: (02) 565-7025
- Chilefilms Pedro de Valdivia, Avenida Pedro de Valdivia, Providencia 719. Tel: (02) 223-8546
- Cinehoyts La Reina, Avenida Ossa 655.
  Tel: (600) 500-0400. Website: http://www.cinehoyts.cl
- Movieland Mall Portal La Dehesa
  Avenida La Dehesa 1445. Tel: (02) 418-6357
- Multicine Vitacura, Avenida Vitacura 6780.
  Tel: (02) 219-2384

BOOKSTORES

- Books & Bits
  Avenida Apoquindo 6856, Las Condes;
  Tel: (02) 210-9190, 210-9100 or 229-9026
  Website: http://www.booksandbits.cl
- Librería Inglesa
  Avenida Pedro de Valdivia 47 #11, Providencia;
  Tel: (02) 231-6270 or 232-8853 and
  at Avenida Vitacura 5950, Vitacura Tel: (02) 219-3080
  Website: http://www.libreriainglesa.cl
- Librería Anglo-Americana
  Avenida 11 de septiembre 2155 #179 (Mall Panorámico).
  Tel: (02) 234-1394

RADIOTAXIS

- Radio Taxi Andes Pacífico. Tel: (02) 204-0104
  Website: http://www.andespacifico.cl
- Radio Taxi Capital Oriente. Tel: (02) 724-8850 or 724-8805
  Website: http://www.capitaloriente.cl
- Radio Taxi Nuevo Flash. Tel: (02) 591-9000
  Website: http://www.nuevoflash.cl
- Radio Taxi Providencia. Tel: (02) 209-0445

MEDIA
Newspapers

- *Santiago Times* (English).
  Website: http://www.santiagotimes.cl
- *El Mercurio*
  Website: http://www.emol.com (see newspapers in
  other cities under 'Diarios Regionales')
- *La Tercera*. Website: http://www.tercera.cl
- *La Segunda*. Website: http://www.lasegunda.cl
- *El Mostrador*. Website: http://www.elmostrador.cl

Television Stations and Cable Companies

- Televisión Nacional de Chile
  Website: http://www.tvn.cl
- TV Universidad Catolica
  Website: http://www.canal13.cl

- VTR
  Tel: (02) 310-1000. Website: http://www.vtr.net
- Direct TV
  Tel: (02) 337-4000. Website: http://www.directv.cl

Radio Channels
- Radio Beethoven 96.5 FM (Classical)
  Website: http://www.beethovenfm.cl
- Radio Cooperativa (News-Music) 76 AM
  Website: http://www.cooperativa.cl
- Radio Zero (Rock) 97.7
  Website: http://www.radiozero.cl

VOLUNTEER ORGANISATIONS
For a complete listing see http://www.fundacionsoles.cl
- Hogar de Cristo (for children, adults and seniors)
  Tucapel Jiménez 44, Santiago. Tel: (188 800) 200-200
  Website: http://www.hogardecristo.cl
- Fundacion Las Rosas (for seniors)
  Rivera 2005. Tel: (02) 737-4394
  Website: http://www.flrosas.cl

RELIGIOUS ORGANISATIONS
(For a full listing of religious organisations, please see
http://www.chipsites.com)
- Saint George's College Chapel (Catholic)
  Services at Santa Maria de Manquehue.
  Tel: (02) 242-6102

- San Marcos Presbyterian Church
  English Service Sunday 9:30 am
  Padre Hurtado Central 599, Las Condes.
  Tel: (02) 224-5893 or 220-2228
  Website: http://www.sanmarcoschurch.cl

- Santiago Community Church (Inter-denominational)
  English Service, Sunday 10:30 am
  Avenida Holanda 151, Providencia.
  Tel: (02) 232-1113

- International Bible Church
  Hotel Kennedy. English Services Sunday 9:30 am
  Avenida Presidente Kennedy 4570, Vitacura.
  Tel: (02) 218-1526

- Sabbath Services Estadio Israelita
  Services in Hebrew and Spanish Friday 7:30 pm
  Avenida Las Condes 8361, Las Condes.

BUSINESS ASSOCIATIONS
- Chilean American Chamber of Commerce (AMCHAM)
  Website: http://www.amchamchile.cl
- Chilean Canadian Chamber of Commerce
  Website: http://www.chile-canada-chamber.cl
- Chilean British Chamber of Commerce
  Website: http://www.britcham.cl

EXPAT ORGANISATIONS
- American Association of Chile
  Chesterton 7579, Las Condes. Tel: (02) 220-3793
  Website: http://www.aachile.org
- Canadian Association of Chile
  Website: http://www.geocities.com/cachile
- British International Group
  Website: http://www.chipsites.com
- International Professional Woman's Association
  Website: http://www.ipwasantiago.org
- Chilespouses (a group for foreigners married to Chileans)
  Contact cathy.casanga@gmail.com

USEFUL WEBSITES
- http://www.chileangovernment.cl (Chilean Government
  website with links to all public entities)
- http://www.chileinfo.com (website of the Chilean
  foreign trade office)
- http://www.chile-usa.org (website of Embassy of Chile
  in the USA)
- http://www.visit-chile.org (website of the Chile Tourism
  Promotion Corporation)

- http://www.sernatur.cl (website of Chilean National Tourism Service—SERNATUR)
- http://www.turistel.cl (travel guide)
- http://www.chipsites.com (general information on everything)
- http://www.contactchile.cl (variety of services for those going to Chile)
- http://www.allchile.net (great place to ask any question on Chile: forums in English on many topics)
- http://www.gochile.cl (information on travel in Chile)
- http://www.chile-travel.com (travel information)
- http://www.chileaustral.com (guide to Chilean Patagonia)
- http://www.torresdelpaine.com (guide to the Torres del Paine National Park)

Municipalities
Each municipality has its own website, for example:
- http://www.santiago.cl
- http://www.lascondes.cl
- http://www.vitacura.cl

Gay and Lesbian Websites
- http://www.gaychile.cl
- http://www.movilh.cl
- http://www.santiago.queercity.info

Chilean Culture
- http://www.nuestro.cl
- http://www.beingindigenous.org
- http://www.islandheritage.org

On-line Sales and Auctions
- http://www.elrastro.cl
- http://www.mercadolibre.cl

FURTHER READING

POLITICS AND HISTORY

A Nation of Enemies: Chile under Pinochet. Pamela Constable and Arturo Valenzuela (W.W. Norton and Company, NY: 1991)
- An excellent and easy to read explanation and analysis of the breakdown of democracy in Chile.

A History of Chile 1808 – 2002. Simon Collier and William F. Sater (Cambridge University Press, Cambridge, UK: 2004)
- Two respected scholars present a summary of Chilean history for history students as well as those without much knowledge of Chilean history.

Chile, Pinochet and the Caravan of Death. Patricia Verdugo (University of Miami/North/South Center Press, Miami: 2001)
- Verdugo, a journalist, interviews military officers and victims of torture to understand what happened in Chile during the dictatorship. Her research was used as evidence in the 1990 Chilean Commission of Truth and Reconciliation.

Remembering Pinochet's Chile on the Eve of London 1998. Steve J. Stern (Duke University Press, Durham, North Carolina: 2006)
- The author combines political analysis with oral histories of those on both sides of the Pinochet regime.

Chile: The Other September 11. An Anthology of Reflections on the 1973 Coup. Ariel Dorfman. Pilar Aguilera and Ricardo Fredes, eds. (Ocean Press, Melbourne, Australia: 2006)
- Various left-leaning authors, including Ariel Dorfman, offer their view of the overthrow of Salvador Allende.

Out of the Ashes: Life, Death and Transfiguration of Democracy in Chile, 1883-1988. James R. Whelan (Regnery Gateway, Washington, DC: 1989)
- This is for those who wish to gain an understanding of the pro-Pinochet point of view. Written by a foreigner, this book

combines an economic and political analysis of Chilean history.

Right-Wing Women in Chile: Feminine Power and the Struggle Against Allende 1964-1973. Margaret Power (Pennsylvania State University Press, University Park, Pennsylvania: 2002)

BUSINESS

Welcome to Chile. American Chamber of Commerce, Santiago.
▪ Valuable information on living and conducting business in Chile. Lots of helpful hints on how to settle in.

Doing Business and Investing in Chile: The Price Waterhouse Guide. (PriceWaterhouse Coopers, Santiago, Chile: 2003)
▪ More valuable information for those in Chile on business.

Guide to Business in Chile 1999-2000. Rafael Aldunate. (Inversiones Divisas Limitada, Santiago: 1999)
▪ This guide is privately published in Santiago and contains information on social, economic and political elements of doing business in Chile. It also addresses the main sectors of the economy, explains the regulatory framework and describes selected corporations.

Doing Business in the New Latin America: A Guide to Cultures, Practices and Opportunities. Thomas H. Becker. (Praeger Publishers, Westport, Connecticut: 2004)

TRAVEL AND TOURISM

Chile: A Remote Corner on Earth (Turismo y Comunicaciones S.A., Santiago)
▪ By far the most comprehensive and detailed travel guidebook on Chile. A must for anyone who plans on staying in Chile for any length of time. The English version is sold as one book with a companion guide on adventure tourism. The Spanish version is published in four volumes. It is available in most large bookstores in Santiago and is known as the Turistel.

Insight Guides: Chile. Kerry Mackenzie, Natalie Minnis. (Insight Guides, London, UK: 2004)
▪ Much more than a travel guide, this book provides detailed information on Chilean culture. The beautiful pictures show just how much there is to see and do in Chile.

Chile's Native Forests: A Conservation Legacy. Ken Wilcox (North Atlantic Books, Berkeley, California: 1997)

Desert Memories: Journeys Through the Chilean North. Ariel Dorfman (National Geographic, Washington, DC: 2004.)
▪ Dorfman, a well-know author and playwright, writes about his travels in the north of Chile.

In Patagonia. Bruce Chatwin (Penguin Books, New York: 1977)
▪ An interesting look at the harsh life experienced by settlers in Patagonia. Full of interesting stories and legends; a real treat.

Full Circle: A South American Journey. Luis Sepúlveda. (Lonely Planet Publications, Australia: 1996)
▪ A combination of travel stories and fabulous tales, you can feel, smell and taste the places he writes about.

The Voyage of the Beagle: Carles Darwin's Journal of Researches. Charles Darwin (Penguin Classics, New York: 1989)
▪ For those who enjoy reading about old world travel and are interested in the development of Darwin's theories.

CULTURE AND FOLKLORE

Mapuche: Seeds of the Chilean Soul. (Port of History Museum, Philadelphia, PA, USA and the Museo Chileno de Arte Precolombino, 1992)
▪ An excellent book on the Mapuche, their beliefs, traditions and crafts. One of the very few books available in English on the Mapuche, it can be found at the Pre-Columbian Museum in Santiago.

When a Flower is Reborn: The Life and Times of a Mapuche Feminist. Rosa Isolde Reuque Paillalef. Edited and translated by Florencia E. Mallon (Duke University Press, Durham, North Carolina: 2002)
▪ The political autobiography of Rosa Isolde Reuque Paillalef, a leader in the indigenous rights movement in Chile.

The Mystery of Easter Island, Katherine Routledge. (Cosimo, New York: 2005)
▪ Katherine Routledge travelled to Easter Island in the early 1900s. This interesting book chronicles that expedition.

The Enigmas of Easter Island. Paul Bahn and John Flenley (Oxford University Press, USA: 2003)
▪ In-depth history of the island that dispels famous myths.

The Complete Guide to Easter Island. Shawn McLaughlin (Easter Island Foundation, Los Osos, California: 2004)
▪ This guidebook can help you plan a trip to the island and teach you about its history.

Rapa Nui, Island of Mystery. Georgia Lee (Easter Island Foundation, Los Osos, California: 2006)
▪ The author lived for many years on Easter Island and relates many stories of the people she met there in this book.

Discoveries: Easter Island. Catherine Orliac and Michel Orliac. (Harry N. Abrams, New York, 1995)
▪ Small guide book loaded with history, interesting facts and wonderful photos.

FOOD AND WINE

Wines of Chile. Peter Richards (Mitchell Beazley, London: 2006)

Chile: The Art of Wine. Sara Matthews (The Wine Appreciation Guild, San Francisco, California: 2003)
▪ Beautiful photography.

Tasting Chile: A Celebration of Authentic Chilean Foods and Wines, Daniel Joelson. (Hippocrene Cookbook Library, New York: 2004)

LANGUAGE
How to Survive in the Chilean Jungle. John Brennan and Alvaro Taboada (John C. Saez Ed., Santiago de Chile: 2006)
▪ A fun and complete guide to Chilean slang. A must for those who wish to speak Chileno.

Chilenismos: A Dictionary and Phrasebook for Chilean Spanish. Daniel Joelson ((Hippocrene Dictionary & Phrasebooks, New York; 2005)

POETRY
Twenty Love Poems and a Song of Despair. Dual Language Edition, Pablo Neruda (Penguin Classics, New York: 2006.)
▪ The best-known and best-loved collection of Neruda's early work. It predates his political days and is simply and beautifully an exaltation of love.

Selected Poems of Gabriela Mistral. Gabriela Mistral. V.B. Price, ed. (University of New Mexico Press, Albuquerque, New Mexico: 2003)

FICTION AND MEMOIRS
Chile: A Traveler's Literary Companion. Katherine Silver, ed. (Whereabouts Press, Berkeley, California: 2003)
▪ A collection of stories by Chilean authors. Arranged geographically, the tales provide an interesting insight into the country.

The House of Spirits. Isabel Allende (Bantam Books, New York: 1986)
▪ A captivating story about a Chilean aristocratic family interwoven with historical events.

My Invented Country: A Nostalgic Journey through Chile. Isabel Allende (Harper Collins, New York: 2003)
- Allende delves into many topics, such as Chilean society, history, geography and government in this memoir.

Ines of My Soul: A Novel. Isabel Allende (Harper Collins, New York: 2006)
- The novel blends history and fiction to tell the story of a woman who travels to Chile in the 15th century.

Memoirs. Pablo Neruda (Farrar, Straus Giroux, New York: 2001)
- The poet's autobiography written in the form of beautiful short pieces.

Persona Non-Grata: A Memoir of Disenchantment with the Cuban Revolution. Jorge Edwards (Nation Books, New York: 2004.)
- Although the story takes place primarily during the author's days in Cuba, it does reflect Chilean social and political life.

The Garden Next Door. José Donoso (Grove Press, New York: 1994)
- The story of a Chilean author who, while living in Spain with his wife, fantasizes about the garden next door and the woman who lives there.

Curfew. José Donoso (Grove Press, New York: 1988)
- The story of a Chilean pop idol who returns to Chile after 13 years on the exact day of the death of Pablo Neruda's wife. The book tells of life in Chile during the Pinochet dictatorship.

The Postman. Antonio Skármeta (Miramax Books, New York: 1995)
- The story of a postman who becomes friends with Pablo Neruda in the small town of Isla Negra. It was later made into a movie, changing the setting to Italy.

Clandestine in Chile: The Adventures of Miguel Littín. Gabriel García Márquez (H. Holt, New York: 1987)

▪ Miguel Littin is a well-known Chilean cinematographer. He was forced into exile, but returned illegally during the military dictatorship to make a documentary. García Márquez, famous for his fiction, reverts to his origins as a journalist to recount Littin's experiences.

Mariana and the Merchild: A Folk Tale from Chile. Caroline Pitcher, Jackie Morris (William B. Eerdmans Publishing Co., Grand Rapids, Michigan: 2002)
▪ A children's book with beautiful illustrations that retells a Chilean folktale about a child from the sea.

The Story of the Seagull and the Cat that Taught her to Fly. Luis Sepúlveda (Scholastic, New York: 2002).
▪ A beautiful story for children and adults about keeping your promises.

ABOUT THE AUTHORS

Susan Roraff was born in Chicago, Illinois. She received her Masters degree in Latin American Studies from Georgetown University. Following graduation, she worked at the Latin American Program of the Woodrow Wilson International Center for Scholars in Washington, DC. She then moved to Santiago, where she worked at an economics research organisation. It was during this time that she met her Chilean husband and travelled extensively throughout Latin America. Since then she has lived in Singapore and Vienna, Austria, and co-authored *CultureShock! Austria*. She periodically returns 'home' to Santiago with her husband and two sons.

Laura Camacho, a native of Galena, Illinois, was a Rotary exchange student to Bolivia. She later married a Latin American and studied Psychology at the Catholic University in La Paz, Bolivia for three years. She received a Bachelor of Arts in Psychology and Spanish and a Master's degree in Spanish Literature and Linguistics from the University of Wisconsin-Madison. Laura has lived the expatriate life on four continents, but her heart remains in Latin America.

INDEX

Titles in the CULTURESHOCK! series:

Argentina	Hawaii	Paris
Australia	Hong Kong	Philippines
Austria	Hungary	Portugal
Bahrain	India	Russia
Barcelona	Indonesia	San Francisco
Beijing	Iran	Saudi Arabia
Belgium	Ireland	Scotland
Bolivia	Israel	Sri Lanka
Borneo	Italy	Shanghai
Brazil	Jakarta	Singapore
Britain	Japan	South Africa
Cambodia	Korea	Spain
Canada	Laos	Sweden
Chicago	London	Switzerland
Chile	Malaysia	Syria
China	Mauritius	Taiwan
Costa Rica	Mexico	Thailand
Cuba	Morocco	Tokyo
Czech Republic	Munich	Turkey
Denmark	Myanmar	Ukraine
Ecuador	Nepal	United Arab
Egypt	Netherlands	Emirates
Finland	New York	USA
France	New Zealand	Vancouver
Germany	Norway	Venezuela
Greece	Pakistan	Vietnam

For more information about any of these titles, please contact any of our Marshall Cavendish offices around the world (listed on page ii) or visit our website at:

www.marshallcavendish.com/genref